A DAZZLING STORY OF
ARCHAEOLOGICAL DETECTION*

"Walsh's reconstruction of the search for the apostle is meticulous and convincing, and his theory of why and how the bones were transferred from one underground chamber to another sometime between A.D. 250 to 315—a problem never yet satisfactorily resolved—is likely to be the best explanation we shall get . . . [with] a sufficiency of fascinating photographs, excellent appendices which include charts of the remaining parts of St. Peter's skeleton, and long discursive notes for each chapter. Catholic or no, skeptic or no, you will read it, as I did, in one sitting, and ponder anew the power of a small group of men who can change the world."—*Best Sellers*

"The full extraordinary story is all here, reading like an Agatha Christie thriller, as clue after clue is found and solved . . . Profusely illustrated, Jack Walsh's highly readable work is worth returning to from time to time as it spans the whole history of the Church, from the death of Peter until the bones of the Prince of Apostles were returned to their original tomb by Pope Paul on June 27, 1968, in a simple ceremony."
—*Catholic Herald*

"Walsh . . . [has] done an admirable job of boiling down a mass of technical reports and learned articles into a relatively simple narrative . . . The Vatican, leaning on the voluminous testimony of Dr. Margherita Guarducci, a Roman archaeologist, is convinced it's found the Prince of the Apostles, and so is Walsh."—*Kirkus*

"Walsh's book is a delicious one, inviting the reader to climb down into the bowels of the basilica and thereby to descend twenty centuries to a point in time when the first Christians were living their faith and dying for it."—*Catholic Twin Circle**

"One of the most intrepid archaeological investigations of the modern era . . ."—*Biblical Archaeology Review*

"Walsh writes in a flowing, compact style and keeps the reader's interest from beginning to end . . . it is excellent reading and a fascinating look backward at what might have happened to one of Christianity's most important figures."

—Chattanooga *Times*

"An intriguing story, both for scientific revelations as well as its religious significance."

—*The American Library Association Booklist*

THE BONES
OF
ST. PETER

The First Full Account
of the Search for
the Apostle's Body

JOHN EVANGELIST WALSH

IMAGE BOOKS
A Division of Doubleday & Company, Inc.
GARDEN CITY, NEW YORK
1985

Image Books edition published March 1985 by
special arrangement with Doubleday & Company, Inc.

Library of Congress Cataloging in Publication Data
Walsh, John Evangelist, 1927–
        The bones of St. Peter.
        Bibliography: p. 179
        Includes index.
        1. Peter, the Apostle, Saint–Relics.
I. Title.
BS2515.W28   225.9'24
AACR2
ISBN: 0-385-15039-3
        Library of Congress Catalog Card Number: 80–2883

Bible passages are quoted from the Revised Standard Version.
All photographs, except nos. 8, 8a, and 25, are from the Vatican Archives.
Drawings in the text are based on material in the Vatican's Official Report of
1951. See Selected Bibliography, under *Esplorazioni etc.*

For
TOM and GLORIA
Thomas and Mariann

Preface

 Some extracts from scripture concerning the bodies of the patriarch Joseph, King Saul, and others:

Then Joseph took an oath of the sons of Israel, saying, "God will visit you, and you shall carry up my bones from here." So Joseph died, being a hundred and ten years old; and they embalmed him, and he was put in a coffin in Egypt.

(Genesis 50:25–26)

And the people of Israel went up out of the land of Egypt . . . And Moses took the bones of Joseph with him . . .

(Exodus 13:18–19)

The bones of Joseph which the people of Israel brought up from Egypt were buried at Shechem, in the portion of ground which Jacob bought from the sons of Hamor the father of Shechem for a hundred pieces of money; it became an inheritance of the descendants of Joseph.

(Joshua 24:32)

———

When the inhabitants of Jabesh-gilead heard what the Philistines had done to Saul, all the valiant men arose, and went all night,

*and took the body of Saul and the bodies of his sons from the
wall of Beth-shan; and they came to Jabesh and burnt them there.
And they took their bones and buried them under the tamarisk
tree in Jabesh, and fasted seven days.*

(1 Samuel 31:11–13)

*David went and took the bones of Saul and the bones of his son
Jonathan from the men of Jabesh-gilead, who had stolen them
from the public square of Beth-shan . . . And they buried the
bones of Saul and his son Jonathan in the land of Benjamin in
Zela, in the tomb of Kish his father.*

(2 Samuel 21:12, 14)

———

*As Josiah turned, he saw the tombs there on the mount; and he
sent and took the bones out of the tombs, and burned them upon
the altar, and defiled it . . . Then he said, "What is yonder
monument that I see?" And the men of the city told him, "It is
the tomb of the man of God who came from Judah and predicted
these things which you have done against the altar at Bethel."
And he said, "Let him be; let no man move his bones." So they
let his bones alone, with the bones of the prophet who came out
of Samaria.*

(2 Kings 23:16–18)

———

*"Brethren, I may say to you confidently of the patriarch David
that he both died and was buried, and his tomb is with us to this
day."*

(The words of Peter,
Acts 2:29)

Acknowledgments

For various sorts of timely assistance, especially in obtaining materials and in the work of translation, I wish to offer my sincere thanks to the following: Dr. Margherita Guarducci of Rome University; Annamaria Conti of the Italian edition of *The Reader's Digest;* Luciano Belanzoni of Rome; Monsignor H. Monni and Don Michel Basso of the Vatican; Mary Cannizzaro, Robert Goyette, Carol Tarlow, and Virginia Armat; Sterling Library, Yale University; the staff of the Dixon Homestead Library, Dumont, New Jersey.

A special debt of gratitude is owed to all those scholars whose meticulous regard for the facts, and whose sincere attempts to interpret those facts, whether pro or con, have made my own studies so rewarding an experience.

Contents

List of Photographs

Illustrations in the Text

THE BONES OF
ST. PETER

PROLOGUE:

The Announcement

When the man named Simon Peter was brutally executed, some 1,915 years ago in Rome, there passed away one of that small band of historical personalities who deserve to rank as monumental. In history's roll of the great in all fields—religionists, statesmen, philosophers, conquerors, educators, scientists—few others can have lived a life similarly fraught, for so long, with such constant, portentous drama. Beginning so obscurely, so humbly, was anyone before or since ever burdened with so weighty and improbable a task? Assuredly, no other has continued, ages after the earth closed over him, to command such deep regard among living multitudes, generation after endless generation.

In the minds—and hearts—of many people it is no small thing that some part of the mortal remains of this man, through whose living body there flowed the power from Jesus to heal the sick and raise the dead, may still be in existence. Even if he is viewed, as in this case he should be, not in a religious context but simply as the first leader of a movement which was to become a world-altering revolution, the question of the survival of his remains still exerts a powerful fascination. And for just over a decade now, precisely that claim has confronted the world.

In the summer of 1968 it was announced by Pope Paul VI that

the skeletal remains of St. Peter had at last been found and satisfactorily identified. The revered bones had been unearthed some
time before, he said, from the tangle of ancient structures that
lay deep beneath the magnificent high altar of St. Peter's Basilica in Rome. Paul was careful to explain that his statement
rested on long and intensive study by experts, but then he deliberately went further, adding the weight of his own prestige. In
light of the archaeological and scientific conclusions, he said,
"the relics of St. Peter have been identified in a manner which
we believe convincing . . . very patient and accurate investigations were made with a result which we believe positive."
Firmly persuaded as he was, he had felt it nothing less than a
duty to make "this happy announcement" at the earliest possible
moment.

The circumstance that the bones were found under the basilica occasioned no great surprise, since the age-old tradition of
the church had always located the original grave of the apostle
just here. Yet to find that after so achingly long a time, and
against all reasonable expectation, some part of this precious
body should still be preserved, seemed incredible, a fit occasion
for rejoicing. The day following the Pope's announcement, in
solemn ceremony led by Paul himself, the bones were restored to
their ancient resting place. Since then, privileged visitors have
regularly been allowed to enter the small, silent chamber beneath the high altar to pay homage to the Prince of the Apostles.
Through a narrow opening in the repository, the bones themselves encased in several transparent receptacles, are just visible.

In releasing his statement, Paul had purposely kept to the essentials of the matter, leaving the details to be supplied to journalists and others by Vatican officials and those directly concerned in the discovery. When the full story reached print,
however, in newspapers around the world, there was immediate
and widespread puzzlement. In place of clarification there arose
annoying clouds of confusion. At fault, to a large degree, was
the intricate mass of archaeological data to be absorbed. But far
more significant was a single hugely surprising fact: the bones
had not been recently discovered, as the Pope had seemed to

imply. On the contrary, they had first been found nearly thirty years before.

There was no attempt to make a secret of this rather astounding development. In fact, all those involved went to some length to make it known, and to explain the circumstances. But here, especially, scholarly thoroughness was much too slow-footed for the hurrying pace of daily or weekly journalism. Even the perplexing, not to say startling admission that, at first, the bones had lain neglected, in some vague way "forgotten," proved inadequate to hold the attention of the press—it could not watch even for an hour, but fell asleep on one of the most compelling scientific stories of the century. All too soon, the topic began fading back into the nether world of the professional journals and monographs from which Paul's declaration had so dramatically called it.

Inevitably, after that first flurry of excitement, and as a direct result of the subject's confusion and difficulty, a reaction set in among the general public. Nagging doubts surfaced even in those initially well disposed, and there came a slackening of interest. Belief or disbelief thereafter was based not on the evidence, but largely on personal proclivity. Among most Catholics, free to decide the question as they wished, there was a natural desire, buoyed by the Pope's assurances, to accept authenticity. Among most Protestants, sensitive to the oft-debated question of the exact nature of Peter's primacy in the church, there was a tendency quite as natural to reject.

In subtler form, and perhaps more or less unconsciously, these attitudes infected even the discussions among scholars, on both sides. Thus, a question which should have been tested on purely rational and scientific grounds, was soon awash in emotion, sinking steadily into scriptural and historical argument. Veiled by the disagreement, the physical evidence was virtually ignored. With the pieces of the puzzle scattered broadcast over this rough sea of contention, the full consecutive story, told in a form readily grasped by the interested layman, never managed to emerge. The inherent fascination of the discovery itself, the intriguing step-by-step progress of the original quest, was all but blotted out.

It was in some hesitation that I made my initial approach to the subject, wary of its bulk and complexity, questioning whether it would really be possible to lift it out of the academic realm. Very soon I saw that if a coherent picture were to be drawn, the presentation must be by way of a true narrative, not a mere synthesis of results, accompanied by analysis and background. At bottom, the search for Peter's relics, while strictly an archaeological endeavor, was in many ways untypical, even unique. Intimately concerned in it, and quite unexpectedly, was an element of human failing, an unfortunate clash of personality and outlook, which in the end had given rise to some strange twists indeed. Only a consecutive narrative, it seemed, permitting the reader to tread in the footsteps of the original excavators, could hope to do justice to the whole truth.

But that reasonable conclusion, I soon saw, made imperative a more measured approach to the subject's rather daunting scholarship. A judicious sifting was called for, through those myriad details of secular art and architecture, cultural and church history, classical studies, legend and the like, which had crept like jungle growth around the story's essential core, screening it from all but the most determined pursuers. For my purpose, the directly pertinent, clearly relevant facts, derived wholly from primary sources and set down without reserve or embroidery, must be allowed to tell their own tale. Of course, in my Notes, an integral part of the presentation, I could treat such scraps of technical argument or scientific detail as might have some random interest or value. Herded safely at the book's close, however, these sometimes involuted and prickly matters would molest no reader inclined to skirt them.

Pope Paul, in making his 1968 announcement about the bones, took care to stress his personal hope and expectation that, despite his public declaration of their authenticity, study of the relics and their background would not cease. There was still much to be learned, he meant, about the darker corners of the long and involved history of the apostle's grave and mortal remains. My own study was not very far advanced before I too began to sense that, even after so many years of scholarly fine-combing, some important aspects of the story still seemed provokingly awry. Thus, as the conclusion to my factual account of the search for Peter's relics I have, in a final chapter, "The Ancient Silence," ventured to offer a few suggestions of my own. It was an added satisfaction, to me at least, that these refinements also threw over the vexing shadows of early Christianity a quite tantalizing, if momentary, flash of light.

My soul shall rejoice in the Lord,
exulting in his deliverance.
All my bones shall say,
"O Lord, who is like thee . . ."

Psalm 35:9–10

I

Buried Tombs

The great central aisle of St. Peter's Basilica in Rome, awesomely flanked by a parade of massive pillars, adorned with monumental statuary, stretches nearly four hundred feet from the main entrance before reaching the majestic high altar, just under the tiered magnificence of the soaring dome. Proportioned on a truly gigantic scale, this renowned promenade offers an unforgettable, soul-stirring vista unmatched anywhere in the world. Like a reverse image of these sweeping splendors, one level below the lustrous marble pavement of the central aisle there lies the cavernous burial crypt known as the Sacred Grottoes. It was in the somber atmosphere of this lower level that the search for St. Peter began, but entirely by accident. At the start there was no hint that a journey back through the ages, even to the morning of Christianity, was imminent.

A long, unusually low-ceilinged chamber, the Grottoes were divided into three broad aisles by a series of squat archways. Sunk into the main walls on either side were the open-fronted crypts in which rested the ornate sarcophagi of many illustrious dead. Among them were the tenth-century emperor of Germany, Otto II, the only English pope, Hadrian IV, who reigned in the twelfth century, Queen Christina of Sweden, and James II of England. It was another burial, that of Pope Pius XI, who died in February 1939, and the alterations needed for his interment, that caused the first extensive change in the area after it had lain undisturbed for centuries. Soon after the Pope's burial it was decided that the Grottoes should be converted to a more practical use, made over into a subterranean chapel. Long contemplated, the move had always before, for one reason or another, been postponed.

Ponderously vaulted, the low-slung ceiling of the Grottoes, allowing only an irregular eight feet or so of headroom, presented the renovators with their first major problem. As the only feasible solution, it was decided to lower the level of the entire floor, or most of it, by some three feet. This proved a formidable task, calling for a prodigious amount of labor, and for several weeks the rude sounds of sledgehammer, crowbar, and winch filled the brooding chamber. At length, when a sufficient portion of the heavy marble pavement and its underpinning had been taken up, the diggers moved in.

Almost immediately the workmen's shovels probing the underlying soil began to uncover a random series of marble and stone sarcophagi, some small and plain, others large and impressively ornamented. These were recognized as burials which had been let down through the flooring at various times in the distant past and they were lifted out for disposal elsewhere, with the older and more interesting ones being set aside for study.

Operations had been in progress for perhaps three months when a digger, starting work on a new location in the south aisle, reported an unusual find. About two feet down he had struck what appeared to be the ragged top of a brick wall. More than a foot thick, it descended into the hard-packed earth to an unknown depth. One side was plain reddish brick, somewhat weathered. The other side held a plaster facing painted a rich greenish-blue.

Under the watchful eye of a Vatican archaeologist, hastily summoned, the whole length of the wall along the surface was laid bare, and it was seen to form one side of a large quadrangle, twenty-two feet by twenty. Even a cursory look showed that the find promised to be exciting: the walls undoubtedly formed

the top of a small building, but the whole roof had been roughly
sheared off, and the remaining shell had been rammed full of
earth. The brickwork, judging by its form and layering, was extremely ancient.

Guided by the archaeologist, diggers began emptying the little
building of its burden of packed soil and slowly, foot by foot,
the level dropped, gradually revealing more of the greenish-blue
plaster. Farther down there came to light an elaborate arrangement of wall niches, some holding cremation urns. The building
was a tomb.

All of the niches, most of them roundheaded with scallop-shell
designs, were painted a dark purple and framed by diminutive
white columns, while a contrasting bright red overspread the adjacent surfaces. Floral decorations, daintily modeled in white
stucco, clung to the walls, in some places with stucco dolphins
sporting among the flowers. In the upper portion of one large
semidomed niche there was a painting, well executed though
somewhat damaged, of Venus rising from the sea. Another niche
held a picture of an ox and a ram at rest in an idyllic landscape,
and in still another there was a miniature stucco frieze, strung
on a scarlet background, of cranes and pygmies. Everywhere the
walls were adorned with a masterful display of pediments, pan-
eling, apses, and entablatures. The entrance doorway, still ele-
gantly framed by fine slabs of travertine (dressed limestone),
faced squarely toward the south side of the basilica. The tomb
itself, in its entirety, sat a bit to the left of the basilica's longer
axis.

After the diggers had removed most of the earth from the
tomb's interior, some six thousand cubic feet of it, the floor was
reached, fifteen feet down, and here a touching discovery was
made. While all of the formal burials in the mausoleum had
proved to be cremations, and thus of pagans—at least a dozen
with inscriptions were ranged along the walls—laid into the floor
was an oblong marble slab which told the excavators that they
had come upon the grave of a Christian.

In the grave, declared the Latin epitaph inscribed on the slab,
lay the body of a woman named Aemelia Gorgonia, a beloved

wife who had been remarkable both for beauty and for inno-
cence, and who had died young. Her age was given as twenty-
eight years, two months, and twenty-eight days. The words *dor-
mit in pace* appeared, using the earliest, and now long-forgotten
form of the familiar *requiescat in pace*. Someone, perhaps the
bereaved husband himself, had painstakingly scratched a simple
scene into the upper left corner of the slab, showing a woman
with a bottle about to draw water from a well. Above the sketch
were cut the words *anima dulcis Gorgonia* (sweet-souled Gorgonia). Together, the words and the drawing, a familiar motif in
early Christianity, expressed the firm belief that the lamented
woman was enjoying the refreshment of heavenly repose.

A little later, while the workmen were clearing earth from the
outside of the tomb, they came upon another isolated burial, this
time of a high-ranking pagan woman. On the ground against the
front wall, just to the left of the door, lay a large sarcophagus,
richly carved from costly Proconnesian marble. The inscription
identified the body within as that of a certain Ostoria Chelidon,
wife of an Imperial official and daughter of a Roman senator
who had filled the high post of "consul designatus."

Gently raising the heavy lid, which was loosely placed, the
searchers saw lying in the shallow trough the partially decayed
remains of a skeleton. Around the skull, like filigree, were traces
of a golden netting, and clinging to some of the bones of the
lower limbs were pieces of moldering purple fabric (a color reserved by Roman law for the apparel of the ruling class). En-
circling the bones of the left wrist, glinting in the light of the
searchers' lamps, was a thick bracelet, apparently of pure gold.
As the men gazed at the pitiful remains, which must once have
presented a truly splendid appearance, they could not help
drawing a contrast with the simple joy which still clung like
an aura round the unassuming grave of the young Christian
wife. In a hush they replaced the lid, thinking that for so important a burial the casual location was strange. But there was no
clue to explain it.

The age of the large tomb was soon determined, causing some
astonishment. It had been built sometime in a twenty-year pe-

riod centering on A.D. 150, and had been in use for almost two
hundred years. According to the numerous inscriptions, it was
the property of a family named Caetennius, members of Rome's
freedman class and evidently of some wealth. While the earliest
burials, those in the urns, were all cremations, it was found that
at a later stage some bodies, in terracotta coffins, had been laid
into arched recesses along the bottoms of the walls. This agreed
with the known fact that burials among the pagans of Rome
during the third century, accompanying a vague but growing
belief in an afterlife, had gradually altered from cremation to
inhumation.

Standing in the cleared interior of the tomb, gazing up in
wonder at its gorgeously decorated walls, which were now a
good deal chipped and faded, the Vatican archaeologists felt a
justifiable pride, even excitement. An accident of fate had en-
abled them to recover what was clearly one of the rarest, best-
preserved examples of funerary architecture remaining from the
height of Rome's golden age. It was a prize well worth the
months of effort, one which was bound to yield much valuable
information after study by specialists. Meantime, it was thought,
the workmen could be returned to the original task of lowering
the Grotto floor.

But the discoveries under the basilica were only beginning.
Diggers, working around the exterior of the Caetennius tomb in
order to free it completely, had uncovered new walls. On either
side, it was certain, there stood another mausoleum, each also
roofless and packed with earth.

While the size and splendor of the excavated tomb, and its
age, had prompted some amazement, its mere presence under St.
Peter's had not been a complete surprise. That pagan burials
of some kind lay under the basilica had long been believed, and
there existed support for the claim in the Vatican's old records,
where accidental discoveries, made while altering or repairing
the church's interior, had occasionally been reported. These
early finds, however, had all come long before there was any
real understanding of archaeology, or even any interest in the

subject. The old reports, colored by the intensely personal views and hearsay evidence of a more impressionable age, offered scant description and few details. Never closely studied, such haphazard discoveries had gone unvalued for whatever information they might yield about the past.

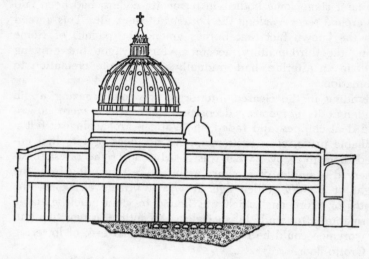

1. Side view of the basilica showing approximate extent and depth of the excavations. The slope from left to right follows the ancient line of Vatican Hill.

One seventeenth-century tale, for instance, told of a large marble sarcophagus, sumptuously carved, which had been dug up in the vicinity of the high altar. Its occupant had proved to be one Flavius Agricola, whose figure in bas-relief reclined full-length on the heavy lid. There was also a long inscription in which the joys of appetite were openly celebrated, offering Agricola's advice to those he had left behind. "Mix the wine, drink deep," it said in part, "and do not refuse to pretty girls the sweets of love, for when death comes earth and fire devour everything." So offended were the authorities by this blatantly pagan sentiment that they promptly had the lid smashed to pieces and thrown into the Tiber.

Another old story, relating to some floor alterations in the year 1574, told how workmen accidentally broke through the top of some vaulted brickwork to find a diminutive pagan tomb. The walls and ceiling, supposedly, were entirely decorated with a beautiful mosaic of gold, and there was a picture which showed a wonderful pair of prancing white horses. Earth and bones filled the lower half of the chamber, and atop the dirt was a slab of marble on which lay a human body covered with quicklime. After a hasty look the intruders had withdrawn. The body was left undisturbed, the opening closed and the tomb given back to the darkness.

Taken together, the old accounts strongly suggested that beneath the modern edifice there lay an actual pagan graveyard, though indeterminate in nature, extent, and date. If this were true, it had always been thought, especially if any of the burials had been the first occupants of the site, then they would have to be very ancient indeed.

The large tract of land that today lies hidden beneath St. Peter's Basilica—in the old Roman district known as Vaticanum—has been sealed off from human sight for more than sixteen hundred years. About A.D. 330, only two decades or so after the Emperor Constantine issued his Edict of Milan, by which he ended the persecution of the infant church, the land was covered by a huge Roman basilica. No doubts have ever existed as to the purpose of this splendid structure—it was built to honor and preserve what was confidently believed to be the true grave of Simon Peter, Prince of the Apostles. Constantine himself, though he was at that period more concerned with the plans for his new capital at Constantinople, took a symbolic part in the work, going so far as to carry on his shoulders twelve baskets of earth-fill, one for each of the apostles.

Thereafter, for the remarkable span of well over a thousand years, Old St. Peter's stood as the acknowledged focus of world Christianity. Annually, down through those centuries, the grave-shrine continued to draw an unfailing and ever-growing throng of the faithful on pilgrimage, a phenomenon unlike anything previously known in antiquity. Then, in the sixteenth century, its very fabric grown decrepit beyond further repair, the venerable structure was taken down, stone by stone. In its place, even while the work of demolition proceeded, there slowly arose—more than a century was needed for completion—an even larger and grander monument, the present basilica with its breathtaking proportions and majestic dome.

Only where digging was necessary to sink foundations for the massive pillars and the enormous walls had the builders of the new church interfered with the original ground. The subterranean grave of Peter, deep beneath the high altar, they had scrupulously avoided. Aboveground, the shrine's superstructure was redesigned, and a more imposing high altar was installed atop a broad, stepped platform. Looming in classic grandeur over the new high altar there rose an elaborate metal canopy carried on four immense pillars, each of which was cunningly twisted along its length so that it resembled a stack of barley sugar.

The floor of the new basilica's central aisle was raised well above the old one, and it was at this time that the Sacred Grottoes were formed on the lower level. Thus, while Constantine's church had completely disappeared aboveground, at no time had there been any wholesale intrusion on the sequestered precincts below. Whatever was buried under the first basilica in the fourth century—no actual record had come down to the present—must still lie there for the most part undisturbed in the twentieth.

2

Street of the Dead

With the discovery of the two new tombs, and the strong possibility that if three stood in a row there might well be others, the work of lowering the Grotto floor was abandoned.

Though the proper excavation of two large tombs, possibly more, would be a large undertaking, there could be no thought of ignoring the finds, of simply burying them anew. Aside from the irresistible scientific lure they offered, there was the definite chance that something of significance might be learned about Peter's own death and burial. His grave under the high altar lay at about the same depth as the Caetennius tomb, and scarcely eighty feet distant.

An excavation team was now formally assembled, consisting of four eminent members of the Papal Institute for Christian Archaeology: two Jesuit priests, Antonio Ferrua and Engelbert Kirschbaum; the Vatican architect, Bruno Appolonj-Ghetti; and the leading authority in the field, Professor Enrico Josi, Inspector of the Catacombs. Nominal leader of the team, by virtue of his office, was Monsignor Ludwig Kaas, Administrator of St. Peter's Basilica. Though not an archaeologist, Kaas was a recognized scholar. German by birth, he had served in the Reichstag before the rise of the Nazis. His administrative skills, resourcefulness, and enthusiasm for the project, as his colleagues later attested, were to prove indispensable to the operations.

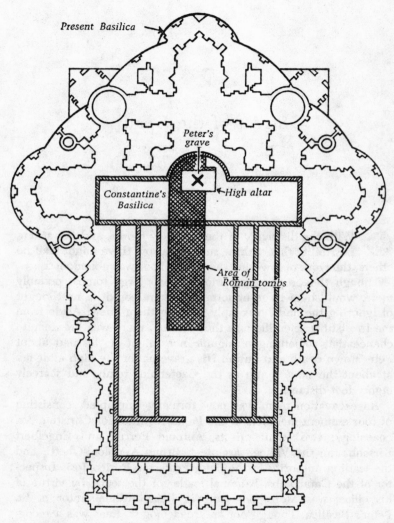

Present Basilica

Peter's grave

Constantine's
Basilica

High altar

Area of
Roman tombs

2. Outline of the present basilica showing comparison with Constantine's fourth-century basilica and site of the excavations. Only a portion of the Constantinian walls was uncovered.

Permission for the enlarged excavation had readily been obtained from the new pope, Pius XII (Eugenio Pacelli), who alone held the authority. He imposed only one condition: while the archaeologists might dig without hindrance under the body of the church, they were not to encroach on the area beneath the high altar. Even attuned as he was to the spirit of modern science, Pius XII was not yet ready to allow an invasion of Peter's grave, so long kept inviolate by his predecessors.

Early in 1941 several diggers began emptying the packed earth from the new tombs, while other men explored around the perimeters. A few days' probing was sufficient to establish the presence of two more tombs flanking the first three. Apparently they were intact, though also roofless and dirt-filled. With this, the excavators agreed that most of the effort should be concentrated to the west of the Caetennius tomb, in the direction leading to the high altar.

Though it proved to be much smaller than the first, the second tomb required a full three weeks to clear, and it yielded only pagan cremation burials. Bright floral paintings and graceful stucco figures decorated its walls, though not in such fine profusion as those of the Caetennius. Dominating the interior, from the top of a niche facing the door, was its sole feature of more than usual interest: a large painting portraying a master in lively converse with a steward. Sitting at a small table, the master holds an open scroll, his right hand raised in emphasis. Facing him is a diminutive white-clad adult, one hand holding a ledger, the other with fingers outstretched as if counting. Evidently a memorial to the tomb's owner, the animated scene probably recorded a lifelong devotion to professional duties. The tomb's date, as anticipated, matched that of the Caetennius, though perhaps a few years earlier.

Eagerly the team pressed on to the adjacent building, and after nearly two months of digging they were rewarded by one of the most remarkable sights that anyone had yet seen from Roman antiquity.

Belonging to a family of wealthy freedmen named Valerius,

the third mausoleum contained no paintings, but built into the vibrantly colored walls were more than a dozen niches, all unusually tall and elaborate. Each niche, gracefully framed, held a single full-length figure modeled in white stucco. Sculpted in high relief and fine detail, the tallest figure stood just over five feet. Both men and women were represented, as well as several gods and goddesses. From one niche, Hypnos, the bat-winged god of sleep, stared stonily. From another, Isis, the great Egyptian mother-goddess who had been adopted by Rome, cast her comforting gaze.

Most of the statues proved to be portraits, showing actual members of the Valerius family who had lived and died during a century or more, about A.D. 130 to 230. In the east wall, in a broad, roundheaded niche, stood the tomb's founder, Gaius Valerius Herma, clad in rich drapery. Occupying the place of honor in a niche facing the entrance was a stately cloaked figure, probably representing Herma's father or grandfather.

Everywhere on the walls appeared more stucco figures, all in exquisite miniature, portraying a bacchanalian festival. Leering Satyrs with tufted beards crouched expectantly. Maenads with flowing garments paraded and danced to clanging cymbals, with torches held aloft. Numerous Pans hurried in frolic to the prancing tunes of their own double pipes. So wonderfully free and flowing was the modeling of these small figures that the technique struck the excavators more as drawing than sculpture. At other points on the walls, in strange and stunning contrast to the revelers, trim-bearded men, akin to the austere figures that would adorn medieval churches, stood as silent reprovers of the wild behavior around them.

Two Christian graves were found in the Valerius tomb, one of them belonging to a man with the ringing name of Flavius Statilius Olympius, whose friends had obviously recalled him with special fondness. "He had a joke for everyone," read his inscription, "and he never quarreled."

Lying loose in the soil, three broken statue heads were turned up, of a man, a woman, and a boy. The mantled head of the woman, made of marble, was especially striking. The lift of the chin, the delicate contour of the high cheekbones, the sensitive lips, the lidded eyes, all combined to produce an expression of noble beauty, subtly overcast by an air of tender sadness. The head of the boy, a tiny stucco piece gilded over, probably portrayed the son of Herma himself. An inscription elsewhere in the tomb revealed that the boy had died at the age of four.

In its technical skill and ambitious treatment, the marvelous display of stucco art in the Valerius tomb exceeded even the best examples previously found anywhere. Here was almost a complete museum of the difficult art as practiced in ancient times. Yet it was not this unique profusion of statuary that gave the excavators their greatest reward in the Valerius tomb. That came when a workman, clearing the heaped dirt away from the curving wall of the central niche, uncovered the first mention of Peter.

Sketched in the plaster beside the right leg of the cloaked figure were two outline drawings of men's heads, one above the other. Drawn in red lead and traced over in charcoal, they were the spontaneous effort of an untutored hand, with shapes and proportions wrong, and thin lines marking eyes, nose, and mouth. The upper head was that of Christ, identifiable by the form of a phoenix—the bird of ancient myth which rose to life from its own ashes—scratched on the forehead, along with the word *vibus* (living). The lower head, showing an older, bald-headed man with wrinkled brow and perhaps a beard, did not carry any identification on itself, but underneath in a half dozen uneven lines of crude lettering there ran a Latin inscription. While only the first few words could be read, these were unmistakable: "Peter pray Christ Jesus for the holy . . ." The rest of the words trailed off, with letters faded or missing, into the confusion of the cracked and mottled plaster.

Such an overtly Christian inscription standing openly among pagan burials was curious, to say the least. Its impulsive character and its random location were also puzzling. Though not by any means the only example of an ancient graffito invoking the apostle, it was the only one accompanied by a drawing. Was its presence here, so close to the traditional site of Peter's grave,

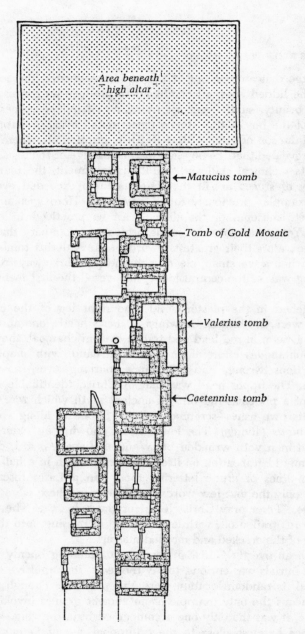

3. The succession of second- and third-century Roman tombs leading toward the high altar. The line of tombs actually extends much farther in both directions, but excavation of the extremities would interfere with the basilica's foundations.

purely an accident? The excavators felt sure that the full inscription, if only it could be deciphered, would supply information of great value: pray for the holy *who* or *what?* But after much effort, the latter half of the scrawl was grudgingly deemed unreadable.

With workmen exploring ahead as well as to the sides, evidence had steadily mounted of the presence of further structures, and it now appeared certain that the line of tombs did extend all the way to the high altar. In addition, the diggers had found indications of more buildings in the opposite direction, to the east of the Caetennius tomb. Even more excitingly, they had also uncovered definite signs of a second line of tombs, paralleling the first, on the south side. The two rows appeared to be separated only by the width of a narrow street.

The old belief about Peter's body resting in the midst of a formal pagan cemetery, it seemed, had not been wrong. Yet the further implications of the tradition—that Peter's actual burial had taken place within an existing pagan graveyard—were still in doubt. None of the three tombs so far dug up could be dated before the middle of the second century, some seventy or eighty years after Peter's death. Still, at least four unexcavated tombs lay on the straight line between the Valerius mausoleum and the high altar, with several others in the facing row. Dates for these had yet to be determined.

Once emptied, the next tomb in line presented an interior whose upper portions were alive with painted birds. On one wall a stately peacock, accompanied by a red-billed goose, stepped grandly through a rose-filled garden, presumably symbolizing the owner's family in the pagan paradise. High on another wall, against a purple field, two elegant snow-white swans stood poised on either side of a large silver candelabrum, a symbolism whose meaning escaped the excavators. Elsewhere, smaller birds of vaguer type perched gaily on borders and pediments. Ranged about the walls were several paintings of stories from Greek mythology, all rather faded. One, better preserved than the others, showed Hercules, with a lion skin and a club on his shoulder, leading the veiled Alcestis home from the grave.

But the tomb's rarest treasure was reserved till last. Spreading itself under the excavators' feet, to cover the entire floor, was a rare black-figure mosaic, done in semi-silhouette, on a white background. The scene depicted was a funerary favorite of the ancients, the Rape of Persephone. Driving a four-horse chariot, the god Pluto controls the reins with his right hand while his left arm grasps a fainting female figure. In front of the horses there hovers in the air the god Hermes Psychopompos, his feet winged, his right hand holding a large serpent-staff. Wrought with enviable skill, the picture was an ingenious adaptation of the legend, making it stand for the rape of the soul by death on its passage to paradise.

The next tomb, a small one, lay directly below the basilica's enormous triumphal arch, the foundations for which had destroyed much of the little structure. Only a few inscriptions remained and these identified it as a second mausoleum of the wealthy Caetennius family.

In the last thirty feet before the high altar two more tombs were unearthed. Another small one, belonging to a family named Aebutius, had also been largely destroyed by foundations sunk from above. Only its façade and part of a side wall had been left standing. The last tomb was larger, almost matching the Valerius in size, but it yielded no surprises nor much of artistic worth beyond some delicate clusters of red and white stucco roses. It had belonged to a family named Matucius, and in one inscription the owner had proudly recorded his success as a dealer in linen.

The excavators now called a halt. Though there was still much to be done, particularly in freeing the tombs of the second row, the work had been allowed to proceed at too rapid a pace. Time was needed for study and review, and for the cleaning up and reorganizing that are a periodic necessity in every excavation. And with that, the most stirring discovery of the entire operation was made.

Between two of the excavated tombs—the second Caetennius and the Aebutius—there stretched an earth-filled passageway, less than ten feet wide. Containing no feature of interest, it had been by-passed in the digging. Now, taking advantage of the lull, the excavators decided to clear it out, starting with a small makeshift grave that blocked the way. Their concern was not with the passageway itself, but with freeing the flanks of the two adjacent tombs. "We let the workmen dismantle and remove an unimportant and unnamed grave," Kirschbaum remembered, "loosely put together with marble slabs, and other remains hardly distinguishable from the dust of centuries. There remained only the ground slab. It was not in our way and we hesitated to get rid of it. Eventually, yielding to a sudden impulse, we had it shifted. To our astonishment, under the slab was an almost circular hole in the ground . . . Workmen lowered a lamp into the darkness and we could make out a small burial vault, half-filled with earth, chalk, and bones. Expectantly, we descended with one of the workmen through the narrow opening."

The chamber proved to be extremely small, only about eight feet in length and height, its width the same as that of the passageway. The dirt-fill, which took up two or three feet of the bottom, further reduced the space. But the crouching Kirschbaum, playing his lamp over the pitch-dark interior, was too entranced by what he saw to be bothered by the cramped quarters.

A mosaic facing of iridescent yellow, which gave back the lamplight in a golden shimmer, covered the whole vaulted ceiling and spread uniformly down over three of the walls to about half their height. Coursing through this glowing background was a luxuriant vine, its wide-clustering mosaic leaves done realistically in several shades of green. It circled the border of the ceiling, then trailed down over the three walls, curling round their centers to frame pictures. Each of the three scenes had been severely damaged by loss of mosaic pieces, but the underlying pattern was clear.

The first picture to greet Kirschbaum's searching light, on the east wall, showed the prophet Jonah falling from the side of a ship, and entering a whale's mouth feet first (an oddity, since Jonah was ordinarily shown being swallowed head first). The second picture, on the north wall, portrayed a fisherman standing on rocks, whose line had already hooked one fish while another swam away. The third, on the west wall, showed the famil-

the Good Shepherd, a sheep laid across his
three subjects were undeniably Christian, and this
tain the interpretation of a fourth picture, which
Kirschbaum's lamp now picked out on the ceiling's glittering
center.

Part of the scene had been destroyed by the opening through
which the men descended, but most of it was intact, and it
clearly portrayed a chariot being drawn through the skies by
two prancing white horses. In the chariot stood a bearded male
figure, his cloak flying in the wind. The figure's right arm was
raised while the lowered left hand held a large globe. Crowning
the head was a nimbus, from behind which there emanated rays
of light, shooting upward and sideways, strongly suggesting the
form of a cross.

Kirschbaum, knowing he was looking at something unique,
could only stare. Here was the pagan myth of Helios, the Greek
sun god, adapted to one of the earliest Christian traditions, in
which the rising and setting of the sun became a dramatic daily
reminder of Christ's Resurrection. This symbolic link between
Savior and sun had been lovingly treated by early writers, but
here in the midst of a pagan cemetery was the only instance of
its use in graphic art, the sole occurrence anywhere of a Christ-
Helios. It was an important discovery, worthy of taking rank
with those other Resurrection symbols from antiquity, Christ-
phoenix and Christ-Orpheus.

After excavation of the chamber had been completed, during
which three Christian burials were located under the floor, the
little tomb gave up the secret of its origin. It had been built toward the end of the second century to hold the ashes of a pagan
child, and its original decoration had been unassuming. About
A.D. 250 the family had been converted to Christianity (or the
tomb had passed to new owners), and in an outburst of spiritual
affirmation it had lavishly redecorated the tomb with the golden
mosaic, the vine, and the pictures.

Besides being the earliest surviving example of a mosaic with
a Christian subject, and the earliest surviving use of crucifixion
symbolism, it was also recognized as the most important artifact,
artistically and technically, to be recovered from under St.

Peter's. Further, the little tomb proved the truth of at least one of the old tales about the basilica. Undoubtedly it was the same one which, in 1574, had momentarily yielded its secret to accidental intruders, except that the body on the slab was missing. How or why it had been taken away, the excavators could only guess.

Some ten months after the start of the excavations, though the work of clearing was still unfinished, the true magnitude of the discovery had become clear. In all, no less than nineteen mausoleums had been located and identified, twelve in the first line and seven in the facing row. Together they held more than a hundred recorded burials, and there were many more interments, some in random sarcophagi, placed in any convenient spot, for which no inscriptions had been provided, or for which none had survived. Most of the dead had come from Rome's freedman class, merchants and traders who had achieved financial success. In many cases, valued slaves had been given a last resting place beside their owners.

The double row of tombs, as unearthed, had an extent of some three hundred feet. But there were definite signs that the original cemetery had extended much farther, perhaps as much as a quarter of a mile. The earliest tomb was the one closest to the high altar, the Matucius, put up about A.D. 125. This tomb, however, had not held the first burials in the area. Several of the other tombs had large ossuariums (bone depositories) built onto their outside walls, a familiar feature in ancient cemeteries. These showed that the workmen in erecting the newer tombs had found it necessary to disturb many earlier graves of a simpler type. As was usual in such cases, the bones from the older earth-graves had been collected, then reinterred as a group in the ossuariums. Peter had indeed been buried in the midst of an existing cemetery, certainly pagan, though it was not the more elaborate one that began to grow up on the site some fifty years after his death.

Aside from the single, half-obliterated inscription in the Valerius tomb, no explicit reference to Peter or his grave had come to light, a grievous disappointment to the excavators. On the other hand, two extraordinary facts did emerge, which together lent dramatic support to the tradition that the apostle's grave lay under the high altar. The first concerned the story mutely told by the buried tombs themselves.

As the excavators established, the entire necropolis had been in regular use until the day, in about the year 330, when the site was taken over for the building of Constantine's basilica. The ancient architects, studying the topography, must have taken special note of one particularly troubling fact—the whole length of the two-rowed cemetery was perched along the side of a hill, up fifty yards or so from a roadway. While the slope was fairly steep from north to south (left to right of the basilica), it was much gentler east to west, in the direction of the double line of tombs. As a result, most of the buildings to the east lay on a descending path, and thus were all at a somewhat lower level than Peter's grave. The architects had made efficient use of this situation. They concluded that the lower tombs need not be demolished, but might simply be buried whole beneath the floor of the basilica. Peter's shrine could then be made to stand above the pavement over the grave, at the place of honor. In addition, if the roofs of the tombs were removed, and the interiors packed with earth, the resulting box-like network of stout walls would serve as extra foundations, helping to prevent slippage of soil on the hillside.

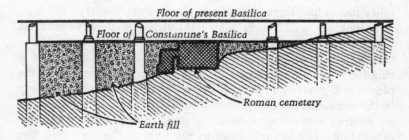

4. Cross section side-to-side (north-south) of the basilica, showing how Constantine's engineers covered the Roman tombs and leveled the slope of the hill. The retaining walls to the left, some thirty feet high, run the length of the building.

But this despoiling of an entire pagan cemetery involved difficulties, both social and legal, which would have given pause even to an emperor. All burials in ancient Rome, from the meanest to the grandest, were very strictly protected by law. Any deliberate "violation of sepulture" was punishable by nothing less than death, and to set aside this prohibition Constantine must have been pressed to invoke the full weight of his imperial powers—indeed, he must have exceeded them considerably. In all Roman history there is no record of any similar action by a ruler against the graves of the Roman citizenry. Even then, Constantine's decision could not have failed to provoke bitter resentment among many pagan families, who at that time in Rome far outnumbered Christians.

The second fact, discovered in the early digging and confirmed by later study, also concerned the hilly nature of the site. Parts of the original foundations of the first basilica had been unearthed, and these told vividly of formidable obstacles overcome. In order to create a broad, flat surface over the face of the sloping hill for the marble pavement of the basilica, at the level of Peter's grave, the builders had found it necessary to construct an artificial platform of prodigious size. Approximately half of it, the half to the south, rested on the natural hillside, but the other half was carried on three enormous foundation walls, running the entire length of the church.

Made of concrete faced with brick, each of the three foundation walls was no less than seven feet thick. At their highest point they rose thirty-five feet above true ground level, and into the huge cavities between them earth had been tightly packed. This earth-moving operation alone, the excavators calculated, would have required the transport of more than one million cubic feet of soil, most of it laboriously carried on the shoulders of workmen, basket by basket, from the hill above. Never suspected before because of later alterations in the terrain, this astonishing fact finally prompted the excavators to label the erection of Peter's first basilica as unquestionably one of the most stupendous construction jobs of antiquity.

With level ground available a few hundred feet to the south, invitingly free of obstruction, why had Constantine gone to such prodigious lengths, borne such great expense, taken the trouble to abrogate rigid laws, in the process alienating many Romans, just to position his basilica in one particular spot on this inconvenient hillside? No visionary, but a ruler notably hard-headed, he was not likely to commit himself solely on the basis of a vague or approximate tradition about the location of Peter's grave. He did have the cooperation of the then-reigning pope, Sylvester, who presumably could have vouched for the authenticity of the site. But it is highly probable that Constantine had also been convinced by some other means, beyond the possibility of doubt, that just here and nowhere else lay the grave into which sorrowing disciples, some 250 years before, had lowered the crucified body of the first pope (transfer of the body itself to level ground was out of the question, absolutely forbidden by the customs of the time).

Did Constantine have the grave opened, did he personally look on the body of Peter? Nothing of this is known with certainty, yet there is evidence—disputed though it may be—that he not only opened the grave but also provided a sumptuous new sarcophagus of bronze, probably lined with gold, for the remains.

Perhaps it was the heady momentum of discovery, intensifying as tomb after tomb steadily carried the excavations ever nearer to the high altar, perhaps it was Pius XII's admitted personal fascination with the question of Peter's grave (influenced, it may be, by the earlier worldwide excitement over Tutankhamen), perhaps it was only a feeling that the time had come. Whatever the precise reason for his bold decision, when the archaeologists suggested to Pius XII that they carry their investigations into the area immediately beneath the high altar, he gave his consent. The age-old tradition about St. Peter's grave was at last to be directly tested.

But the Pope made one firm stipulation: until the work was complete, and a full official report ready for publication, no breath of the results, whatever they might be, should reach the public. All must be accomplished in private and in secret. Readily accepting this condition—not unreasonable in the circumstances—Monsignor Kaas and his four colleagues set to work, never guessing that they were committing themselves to a decade of silence.

3

Beneath the High Altar

Imagine an immense square shaft, say of concrete, twenty feet on a side and measuring some forty feet from top to bottom. Picture this shaft standing upright just beneath the basilica's high altar. Its top touches the undersurface of the broad platform on which the altar rests, the bottom nestles far down in the virgin soil of Vatican Hill. Crowding confusedly round the shaft is an agglomeration of marble hangings, metal partitions, mosaic designs, and brick and mortar walls which run in several directions, at right angles and in curves.

Opening off the shaft's west face, at the rear of the high altar, is a small underground chapel. At the altar's front, the east face, there is a sunken area. This is not covered over by the basilica floor as is the chapel behind, but is open to the view of anyone standing on the main pavement above. Here a large cupboard-like space is let into the face of the shaft, and secluded behind bronze grillwork doors.

In essence, this imaginary shaft describes and delimits the physical problem confronting the archaeologists beneath the high altar: a hoary pile of masonry and other unknown materials, hemmed in on all sides, its mysterious core made up of the structural detritus of past ages. No one in the twentieth century, or for many centuries past, had any real idea of what lay inside this ancient assemblage; no one could say for certain what lay under it.

Early Christian sources supplied scant help, having little to say about the nature or exact location of Peter's original grave, or its subsequent history. Some thirty documents of all sorts had survived from the earliest times, all long pored over by scholars, which treated various aspects of Peter's Roman sojourn and death. But while these supplied strong support for the tradition that he was martyred on Vatican Hill, and had been buried in the immediate vicinity, they told little about the actual circumstances of his death and burial.

Curiously, the New Testament itself offered nothing at all about Peter's final end, beyond the prophecy of Jesus that he would die in old age, a victim of crucifixion. "When you were young," Jesus had told him, "you girded yourself and walked where you would; but when you are old, you will stretch out your hands, and another will gird you and carry you where you do not wish to go." These words of Jesus were reported in the Gospel of John, who comments, "This he said to show by what death he was to glorify God." (The phrase "stretch out the hands" was well understood in antiquity to mean crucifixion.)

Even the book of Acts, which has much to tell of Peter's leadership of the infant church in Jerusalem, maintains a cryptic silence on the matter of his last days and death—in fact, except for one brief reappearance, he simply vanishes, abruptly and rather mysteriously, from its pages. After escaping from prison in the year 43, he pays a hasty visit to Mark's house, leaves certain instructions and, as Acts laconically finishes, "Then he departed and went to another place."

For whatever reason, that other place is not identified, and for the approximately twenty-five years of Peter's life thereafter almost nothing is known with certainty, except that he attended the Jerusalem Council in the year 49, stayed briefly at Antioch and then, soon or late, made his way to Rome. There, during Nero's mad slaughter of Christians following the great fire of A.D. 64, which destroyed a large part of the city, he was executed by crucifixion. Sometime before his death, according to tradition,

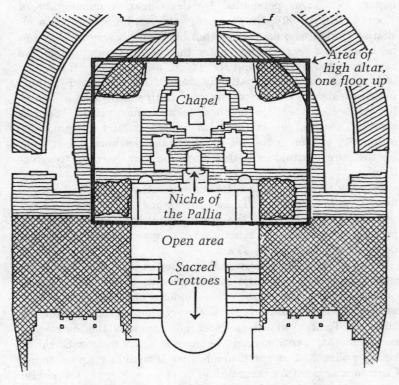

5. Plan (simplified) of the basilica's lower level in relation to the high altar area and the Sacred Grottoes, where the excavations began.

he provided the materials on which Mark's Gospel is based. It is even possible that he reviewed the finished Gospel himself, or an earlier version, and approved it for reading in the churches.

One famous legend asserts that when Nero's persecution first began, Peter was persuaded by the Christian community of Rome to flee the city. On the road, however, he encounters a vision of Christ, who announces that he is on his way to Rome to be crucified a second time. Peter then returns, resigned to the fate predicted by Jesus and for which, during nearly the whole of his adult life, he had patiently waited. That he faced his ultimate ordeal with the serenity born of faith can be seen in one of his last letters, perhaps dictated in a Roman prison. "So put away all malice," he exhorted his followers, "and all guile and insincerity and envy and all slander. Like newborn babes, long for the pure spiritual milk, that by it you may grow up to salvation."

It is said that, at the last, feeling unworthy to die in the same manner as his Master, Peter asked to be nailed to the cross head downward. The date of the event, even after much scholarly probing to determine it exactly, can be given only as sometime between late 64 and mid 68 A.D.

It is just possible, however, that Peter did meet his death, as some maintain, in the first ferocious wave of Christian executions ordered by Nero two or three months after the great fire. If so, then a description left by a near-contemporary, the Roman historian Tacitus, affords a brief glimpse into the harrowing spectacle that accompanied the apostle's last moments. After Nero's police had swept through Rome, rounding up as many Christians as possible, several days were given over to the public executions: "Their death was turned into a diversion. They were clothed in the skins of wild beasts, and torn to pieces by dogs; they were fastened to crosses, or set up to be burned so as to serve the purpose of lamps when daylight failed. Nero gave up his own gardens [circus] for this spectacle." The orgy of slaughter became so revolting even to pagan sensibilities that among many Romans it "aroused a feeling of pity" for the otherwise despised victims.

Surprisingly, details of Peter's burial were also passed over in silence, even in most of the apocryphal writings, where imagination usually was prompt to fill in such oversights. Nowhere in any of the early documents was the location of the grave on Vatican Hill given with a precision which would allow it to be pinpointed. The sole surviving reference to the actual interment, its accuracy very doubtful, occurs in the second-century apocryphal book *Acts of Peter:* "Marcellus, not asking the leave of any, for it was not possible, when he saw that Peter had given up the ghost, took him down from the cross with his own hands, and washed him in milk and wine; and he cut seven minae of mastic, and of myrrh and aloes and Indian leaf fifty, and filled a coffin of marble of great price with Attic honey and laid it in his own tomb." Marcellus was a Roman senator converted by Peter, supposedly, but whether he ever in fact existed, or where his tomb may have been situated, or whether there was any slightest basis of truth in the story at all, remain unanswerable questions.

Within twenty years of Peter's death, according to one source, some sort of "memorial shrine" had been erected over the grave by Pope Anacletus, in apparent and rather surprising disregard of the pagan authorities. At that same time, it was claimed, a burial ground for future popes was also prepared nearby. In any case, that a monument did eventually adorn the grave can be taken as certain because of a chance remark made by a priest named Gaius, a known figure in the early Roman church. About the year 200 Gaius referred, familiarly and in writing, to the "Tropaion" of Peter, which he said was then standing on Vatican Hill. This unusual word, it is now agreed, does indicate a veritable shrine, standing above the actual grave, not a cenotaph, and not simply a marker fixing the place of martyrdom (its closest English equivalent, *trophy,* misses the full meaning and association of the Greek term). When Constantine erected his basilica about a century and a half later, it must have risen above this Tropaion, if it was then still in place.

The bronze sarcophagus supposedly provided by the Emperor for Peter's body was mentioned in documents that went back at least to the fifth century, only some hundred years after the fact.

But there was much disagreement as to the full and true import of these none too clear accounts. Many rejected even the possibility, calling the bronze coffin nothing but a myth, or arguing that, in any case, Peter's remains would never have been disturbed. Others accepted a reburial as possible, perhaps even probable, but they differed as to the form of the bronze coffin. Some saw it as a square chest, about five feet on a side, buried in the original grave. Others pictured it as a large casing, fifteen feet long and nearly ten feet in both height and breadth, situated either above or below ground.

Among the excavators, Monsignor Kaas, who had long studied the question, was inclined to favor the tradition, at least in its essentials. He confidently expected to find a bronze casket, large or small, of whatever design, in or under the pile of masonry. His four colleagues were less sure. So much of precisely this sort of detail in the early non-canonical writings, even in documents otherwise reliable, sprang from hearsay, misunderstanding, or pure exaggeration. Doubts were always justified, especially in the absence of corroboration from independent sources. Peter's body, or his bones, if moved at all, might have been placed in any sort of receptacle, even an urn. Despite the Marcellus legend, it was quite probable, even likely, that the original grave had been no more than a simple earthen trench, several feet below the surface, with the corpse protected by slanting marble slabs in the manner of the poor of the time. Constantine might well have preferred to leave the primitive aura of such a grave unimpaired, erecting his monument over and around it.

What form the aboveground shrine might have taken—rising in the basilica at the juncture of apse and nave—was completely unknown. Concerning only one detail did the excavators feel sure: the shrine must in some way have been centered on a large altar for the celebration of mass, with ample space around it to accommodate the daily stream of visitors. "To this tomb," one eyewitness reported even while the basilica was still under construction, "countless crowds come from all parts of the Roman Empire, as to a great sanctuary and temple of God."

What these throngs saw, or exactly how they went about their

devotions, were matters unrecorded, except for a single tantalizing instance. A sixth-century account, referring to a time when
the early shrine still stood unchanged, describes how a visitor
should conduct himself, providing in the process a fleeting
glimpse of the shrine itself, but telling little about the overall
design. Its reference to a pious superstition of the day may indicate that the grave had not been entirely closed off:

> The man who desires to pray opens the barriers which enclose
> this holy place and comes to the tomb. Then he opens the little
> window, leans his head through it and asks for what he needs.
> He will not have to wait long for a successful answer if he has
> prayed properly. If he would like to have a holy relic, he
> should leave a small cloth there, which he has already had
> weighed. Then he should pray devoutly, with watching and
> fasting, that the apostolic power may come to aid his devotion.
> And then—wonder of wonders—if his faith be strong the cloth
> he draws up from the tomb will be so rich with divine power
> that it weighs more heavily than before, and so he under-
> stands that he has received the grace for which he prayed.

The small cloth, evidently, was let down on a string through
some sort of narrow shaft to make contact with the "tomb,"
whatever that word may here imply. It is also clear from the description that the pilgrim is on a higher level than the grave, but
that perhaps meant little, since he might have had to mount a
platform to reach the "barriers." So close an approach to the
shrine was a privilege probably not granted to everyone.

In later centuries, on several occasions sweeping alterations
were made in the shrine's superstructure. As a result, when Constantine's basilica was finally demolished in the sixteenth century, the form of the central, aboveground shrine could have
borne little resemblance to the original. Three times new high
altars had been installed, the first about A.D. 600 by Pope
Gregory the Great, the second five hundred years later by Pope
Callixtus, the third in the seventeenth century by Pope Clement.
But in exactly what manner all these changes had been accom-

plished, how much of the previous designs were obliterated, and
whether the old altars were removed or left in place, were questions admitting of no certain answers.

Of more concern than the gradual metamorphosis of the
upper shrine was the disturbing fact that on one definite occasion it had been sadly desecrated by foreign invaders. In August
of A.D. 846, a fierce army of Saracens, numbering ten thousand
men, landed in Italy from seventy-five ships and with little op-
position entered Rome. Conquering armies had plundered the
city several times before, but the Saracens, ferocious haters of
Christianity, were the first to vent their wrath on its holy places.
Storming into St. Peter's, destroying and looting, they despoiled
even the high altar. While the records of this melancholy event
are fragmentary, one source employs a phrase of chilling impli-
cation when it asserts that the marauding troops in the basilica
perpetrated "unspeakable iniquities." Whether this meant that
they broke into the space below the shrine, laying impious hands
on the grave itself, no one in later centuries could tell.

When the Saracens, under pressure of Italian troops from
Spoleto, withdrew from Rome and eventually from Italy, their
depradations were soon patched up. For more than a thousand
years thereafter, up to the moment the four archaeologists
mounted their own scientific invasion, the shrine had remained
undisturbed, effectively sealed off from intrusion. Only twice in
all that time—once by accident and once on purpose—had anyone been afforded even a glimpse into its dark interior.

The accident, which happened in 1594, occurred while some
reconstruction was in progress near the high altar. A large piece
of masonry broke from the top of a pillar, plummeted down, and
smashed against an undetermined part of the shrine (the documents mention a vague "floor"). The impact produced a jagged
crack, and some workmen gazing in wonder through the slim
opening were dazzled, as they later claimed, by the sight of a
golden cross. Pope Clement, hastily informed of the damage to
the shrine, immediately ordered the crack closed with cement.
Further work in the vicinity was forbidden.

No proof exists that the men actually saw a golden cross, but that the shrine once included such a rare ornament was a tradition well known to the excavators. When first erected in the fourth century, the monument received from St. Helena, mother of Constantine, a sumptuous gift consisting of a kingly crown and an oversize cross, both made of pure gold. In the early days the crown had been suspended directly above the shrine's center. The sources said nothing definite about the location of the cross.

The second glimpse into the tomb took place at the end of the nineteenth century when a Jesuit historian, Hartmann Grisar, prompted by the development of the electric light, was permitted to try an experiment. His focus was the cupboard-like niche sunk into the east face, in the open area at the altar's front. Known as the Niche of the Pallia (a new bishop's official stole, or *pallium*, rested here overnight before being bestowed), this space contained in its ornate metal bottom a tiny hinged door which opened on a small vertical shaft. Lined with green porphyry, at least in its upper portion, the shaft was very small and narrow, measuring only five by eight inches. Thinking that this could easily be the same shaft through which early pilgrims had lowered their bits of cloth, Grisar let down a feeble electric light.

At a depth of about fifteen feet the light stopped. With his face pressed to the small opening, the anxious Grisar could make out little below except murky shadows, slowly shifting in the yellowish glare of the swaying bulb. He concluded that the shaft opened on a small chamber, apparently measuring only a few feet on a side but perhaps a great deal larger. No object was discernible in the dim circle of light, no gleam of metal. What the chamber might contain, what part of the original grave it represented, or if indeed it bore any connection with the grave at all, Grisar had found it impossible to say.

4

Peter's Grave

Discouragingly, the archaeologists' initial examination of the shrine under the high altar, from all angles and at both upper and lower levels, revealed no easy or preferred way to begin penetration. Moreover, the difficulty of the task had been increased by several new requirements. There was to be no interference with the regular use of the basilica for ceremonial purposes, nor was any power equipment to be employed. The workers must rely on hand tools.

Above all, the archaeologists were not to endanger or destroy any essential parts of the monument. They might probe, breach and dismantle as they wished, but not to the extent of altering or obliterating any of the shrine's main features. When all was done, the area must continue as a vital part of the church above it. Quite ready to struggle with these additional constraints—hampering for any such operation, though in this unique case only sensible—the four set to work. To perform the heavy labor, they were assigned several of the Sampietrini, the Vatican's hereditary corps of workmen.

The small underground chapel opening off the shrine's west face had been fashioned in the sixteenth century, and had been many times redecorated. On the front wall of this chapel (the rear wall of the shrine) there hung a large nineteenth-century mosaic showing full-length, life-size portraits of Peter and Paul on a gilded background. Frame and all, this huge work was detached from its moorings and taken down. Behind it, a plain brick wall was uncovered, the upper half of which was seen to date to the seventeenth century. Surprisingly, the lower part proved to be nearly a thousand years older, dating to the reign of Gregory the Great. This was a formidable barrier and to get past it required going directly through it. After some study, one of the Sampietrini was detailed to hack out several bricks from the upper portion, at its center.

Mortar flew under the sharp chisel, carefully the bricks were worked free, and the excavators found themselves looking at a flat section of white paonazzetto marble. Running up the middle was a narrow strip of rich dark porphyry. With that, the whole outer brick wall, both older and newer portions, was deemed expendable and some days later it had been entirely removed.

The white marble backing covered an area some eight feet broad and more than ten feet high. Dividing it equally in half was the narrow strip of porphyry. At its top, the marble wall disappeared behind the bottom edge of a large altar, which the excavators soon identified as the one installed by Pope Callixtus in the twelfth century.

Since the vertical center strip provided the only way of seeing behind the marble without damaging it, this was now pried loose. Another partition was revealed, this time of mortar. Patiently chipping through the mortar, the workmen uncovered still another wall, but this one showed a plaster facing painted a bright red, now somewhat faded. Tapping gently at the bricks with a hammer, scraping lightly, the workman opened a hole through this red wall, which proved to be made of not one but several layers of brick. Behind, there was only darkness. Kirschbaum, the smallest of the four excavators, stood on a support, inserted a flashlight, and worked his head into the opening. He found himself looking up into the hollow interior of still another old altar, nestled inside that of Callixtus. It was the sixth-century altar of Gregory the Great.

These two old altars, both resting at a somewhat higher level, made the excavators question whether the broad paonazzetto marble slab might not be the remains of a Constantinian altar. Of course, no altar could have been so tall, but the two marble halves flanking the porphyry strip were each of a size and shape which suggested that they could, if repositioned, have been the back and front, or top, of a normal altar. Nothing more could be done at this location without inflicting excessive damage, so the team turned to find some other means of penetrating the shrine.

The side wall of the chapel, just to the right of where the mosaic of Peter and Paul had hung, appeared to offer the best chance of reaching round the shrine, and this wall was soon breached. Behind it a narrow, curving passageway was discovered, little more than two feet wide. Kirschbaum entered, sidled his way along for some ten feet, then found himself standing in a chamber about the size of a large wardrobe closet. There in front of him was the south side of the shrine.

Here also the marble wall was topped by the same Callixtus altar, the bottom edge of which was supported on two small pilasters. But closer inspection showed that this marble section was not of the same type as the piece that hung at the front. It belonged to a much later period, probably the Middle Ages, to which the pilasters could also be dated. Kirschbaum reported his find to the others and they agreed that the medieval wall could be sacrificed.

Two of the Sampietrini entered the confined space and proceeded to remove the marble hanging, no easy task. Then, under Kirschbaum's direction, they began chipping through a series of brick walls. There were four in all, of different thicknesses, and obviously the work of different periods. The fourth wall, very roughly made and evidently very ancient, had already begun to crumble away at its right edge, so the workman discarded his hammer and chisel, picked up a knife, and started scraping at the loose mortar. A few minutes later he announced that he was uncovering still another piece of white marble, and with this Kirschbaum ordered the last brick wall to be taken down entirely. "Expectantly, we turned our attention to the right side," he recalled, "and the crisp sound of the chisel as it splintered the brickwork under repeated hammer blows echoed the tense expectation we all experienced."

What was revealed was both intriguing and puzzling. While the interior appeared to be almost completely taken up by a hard mortar-and-stone fill, several separate features were visible.

At the left could be seen a vertical strip of the red plaster, the reverse of which had been encountered on the chapel side. Here it was faced with marble, at least in its lower half. Just above the marble a thick slab of travertine extended straight out from the red wall, with its forward edge resting atop a small, graceful marble column. Clearly, some sort of deep shelf, almost four feet from front to back, had stood here as an integral part of the structure. Had it been used as an altar? Its height above the original ground, about six feet, seemed to rule that out.

The foundation of the red wall itself went down into the soil well below the pavement around it, deeper even than the level

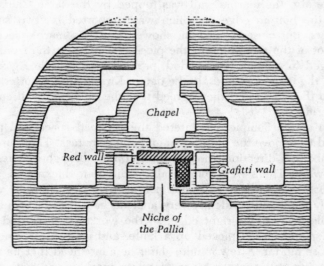

6. Plan (simplified) showing the location of the red wall and the graffiti wall within the structures immediately beneath the high altar. Also shown, just to the left and right of the red wall, are the side chambers found by the excavators.

of the Constantinian floor. Also, the wall was much thicker here than it had appeared from the chapel side, a surprising eighteen inches. Reluctant to interfere with a construction whose nature was still obscure, and which might well be linked to the fourth-century monument, the team now decided to transfer its operations to the opposite side of the shrine.

Back in the chapel, the Sampietrini proceeded to breach the left-hand wall. As anticipated, a similar small chamber was found behind it, giving access to the shrine's northern flank. Again the broad marble hanging was removed, and again a series of brick-and-mortar walls confronted the workmen. Promptly they began hammering their way through each wall in turn, but then, as the face of the innermost wall was uncovered, an exciting difference showed up. It was not rough brick as on the other side of the shrine. Unexpectedly, it carried a facing of light-blue plaster, faded now to a mottled blue-white. Scratched into this plaster was a confused tangle of thin lines which, here and there, formed themselves into recognizable names.

Some hours later, with the wall completely exposed, it was seen that these crude inscriptions occupied an area about three by four feet, nearly the whole of the available space. Running in virtually all directions, there was a regular forest of scratches, pursuing, crossing, leaping over one another, long and short, thick and thin, densely covering almost every square inch of the plaster. It was a strange, patternless jumble of graffiti, and the excavators now saw that many more names were present than had at first appeared.

Crowded against and on top of one another, seemingly without any order, most of the names were legible only in part. Those that could easily be read were all in Latin: Gaudentia, Venerosa, Ursianus, Leonia, Bonifatia, Simplicius, Paulina, among others. The fact that all, or most, were names of persons already dead at the time was clear from the many funerary invocations which accompanied them, such as "*vivatis in Christo*" (may you live in Christ).

Interestingly, Christ's name was nowhere spelled out, but appeared in the form of the familiar monogram, the chi-rho symbol or *labarum*, in which the first two letters of the sacred name in Greek are entwined (☧). It was the presence of this symbol—it appeared at least thirty times and on all parts of the wall —which gave the excavators a date for the graffiti. All must have been scratched into the plaster during a twenty-year period, from A.D. 312 to about 330, when work on the basilica was begun. It was in 312 that Constantine won his final military victory in Rome, at the Milvian Bridge, giving him sole claim to the emperorship, and spreading knowledge of the monogram among Christians. His pre-battle vision of a cross in the sky, along with the words *In hoc vince* (In this, conquer), and his use of the monogram on the shields and helmets of his troops, was well known.

The wall itself, as the archaeologists realized, was a different matter and might easily be much older than these dates. Certain elements of the construction, in fact, placed it in the mid third century, perhaps fifty years before the first graffiti appeared on it.

The one name that the excavators hoped to find on the wall, and eagerly expected to find, was that of Peter. All the inscriptions had quite obviously been made by pilgrims to his grave, where they recorded the names of departed loved ones. That some of these visitors should have invoked the name of Peter as well as that of Christ, the usual practice at the tombs of saints and martyrs, would have been only natural. But search as they might, painstakingly tracing out lines amid all the confusion, they were forced to admit that the name of Peter never once showed up. Greatly disappointed, they still were able to find some consolation in the known fact that there existed in Rome one or two other saints' graves with this same puzzling absence of the principal name.

Lower down on this graffiti wall, about two feet from the bottom, a short strip of plaster had fallen away, leaving a ragged horizontal scar. In some curiosity, the excavators saw that no bricking showed in the aperture where, with the plaster gone, the inner wall should have been uncovered. Shining a light in, they were just able to make out what appeared to be a man-made cavity. The view through the narrow opening was constricted, but along the back there showed a straight edge, dully reflecting the flashlight, and it seemed that the space must be lined all round with marble. To gain entry, however, would mean knocking down more of the plaster, and this would destroy too much of the delicate graffiti crowding round. The team decided it would first make a more careful study at the chapel side of the shrine. They especially wanted to have another look at the red wall, a strip of which was visible at the graffiti wall's right edge.

The suspicion had now strengthened that the broad section of paonazzetto marble, hanging on the chapel side of the shrine, was indeed a part of Constantine's original monument, and even the possibility of this was enough to forestall any attempt to dislodge it. The vertical center strip, with its porphyry covering removed, still gave the only means of access, and by looking through this opening, high and low, with a good deal of squirming and straining, the team was able to establish several points.

The other side of the red wall, at its middle, was not a flat surface. Both above and below the shelf-like travertine slab, semicircular niches had been cut deeply into it, the upper niche being the wider. In the center of the top niche there was a rectangular opening running through from front to back, rather like a small window.

The red wall itself they found to be a decidedly peculiar formation. It was made of a huge rectangular block nearly eight feet high, seven feet wide, and almost two feet thick. Later, after inspecting both ends through slight gaps in the marble, they were able to conclude with certainty that the red wall as it then stood was only a remnant. Its outer corners were not well defined but consisted of an untidy mixture of mortar and brick patching. At either end, it was plain, the red wall had originally extended to unknown distances. Whether it had also once been higher could not be said, since there was no way to inspect its top short of a general dismantling of the entire shrine.

As the excavators knew, in another of Constantine's early

Christian basilicas—the Church of the Holy Sepulcher in Jerusalem—the ancient architects had used an efficient though insensitive approach to the problem of enshrining Christ's tomb. They first pared away all the excess rock surrounding the tomb, and then encased the remaining rock in a sumptuous marble housing. No one in antiquity had objected to this violent—and as modern observers would feel, shudderingly unfortunate—truncation of Christianity's principal physical monument. Was it possible that the same heavy-handed method had been followed at St. Peter's? If so, it was indisputable that this red wall, with its two niches and its travertine table, was the object enshrined. But what relation could the curious structure bear to the apostle's grave? It was at this juncture that the archaeologists first hopefully recalled the remark of the Roman priest Gaius about the "Tropaion" which in the second century had stood on Vatican Hill.

The Pallia Niche, directly on the other side of the chapel wall, it was thought, might offer a different viewing angle, perhaps completing the picture of the perplexing red wall. At first the team had hesitated to interfere with this main feature of the shrine, since it was so integral and living a part of the high altar complex, as well as the portion most visible to the public. Now it was decided to make at least a tentative inspection, and since nothing could be done in that area in the daytime, the team gathered in the basilica after closing on two successive nights.

Within the narrow, arched Pallia Niche, affixed to the walls on either side, were mosaic pictures encased in heavy frames. With some difficulty these were removed. Behind them were older walls, both bearing pictures of medieval saints, now almost faded away. Occupying the whole rear wall of the niche was another large mosaic, of Christ, also dating to the Middle Ages. This impressive and familiar work the excavators felt obliged to leave in place. Nothing else appeared to be detachable without damage, and the searchers had to be content with peering through a narrow gap at the right. They were just able to make out the shoulder of the top niche in the red wall, permitting some vital measurements to be made.

Also in view through the gap was the right-hand portion of the travertine slab, corresponding with the piece discovered previously on the left. The whole center portion of the shelf was missing, however, simply broken out, and into the space between the two remaining margins the present Pallia Niche had been backed. Some close observation made it certain that the travertine shelf had once been a single piece, about five feet wide by four deep. Its height from the ground, about six feet, was also confirmed.

These results, important as corroboration, still left the excavators feeling rather at a loss that the Pallia Niche had failed to resolve more fully the question of the red wall, their efforts blocked by the Pope's sensible admonition to work with all due care. But in another way the party felt itself well requited, since for the first time the four were able to experience in leisurely fashion the basilica's fabled nighttime enchantment. Outside the lone circle of light at the Pallia Niche, Kirschbaum recalled, the lofty ceiling and distant upper reaches of the immense building "merged into the darkness, and the gigantic expanse widened almost to infinity. Wherever the searchlight beam rested for a moment it swam into view, as though touched by an unearthly magic, only to sink back into darkness again. The massive form and figures of this magnificent building dissolved into a rhythm of flow and movement and effulgence, as it were into some silent chorale."

The shrine having been probed on all four sides, it was now time to delve beneath it. For this climaxing operation, eagerly anticipated, it had been concluded that an entry under the graffiti wall, below its foundations, would be best. Some days later the party returned to the small north chamber where the workmen prepared to breach the floor, pausing only long enough to take a closer look at the curious man-made cavity sunk into the graffiti wall.

Gently hammering at the edges of the blue-white plaster, a workman deftly enlarged the aperture. As the hole widened, he reported that there appeared to be nothing inside, and a sweep of a flashlight across the interior confirmed the fact. Except for a lining of marble slabs, and some bits of debris and soil scattered over the bottom, the cavity was empty.

Reaching in, the workman brushed the sparse debris into a pile which he carefully scooped up and lifted out. Spreading the pile on a board, he spotted a coin. Much worn, it was identifiable as coming from the medieval duchy of Limoges in France. Though no date could be read, the excavators agreed that the coin could have been minted no earlier than about A.D. 900, an estimate later proved correct. From the scant pile, the excavators also picked out a few pieces of metal, probably lead, they thought, and several silver threads. Three or four tiny slivers of matter, hard and blackened with dirt, when washed turned out to be splinters of bone, probably human.

The marble-lined cavity itself was larger than expected, extending all the way across the graffiti wall from one side to the other, about three and a half feet. Measuring some ten inches from front to back, it was just over a foot from the bottom slab to the rough top. Whether it was an original feature of the graffiti wall, or had been hollowed out after the wall had been some time standing, was difficult to determine.

The right extremity of the cavity where it abutted on the red wall was not bricked up, and here the red plaster could be glimpsed even fresher and more vivid than on the chapel side. There appeared to be some scratches on it, suggesting more graffiti, but this was uncertain because of the lighting angle, and there was no way to get nearer without breaking off more of the bluish outside plaster. At the moment, that made little sense, since it would only be exchanging one set of graffiti for another. The four were aware that the inscription on the red wall, if such it was, must have been scratched on while the position stood free and unencumbered, and thus would be even earlier than those on the graffiti wall. But they managed to curb their curiosity.

1. Start of excavations in the Sacred Grottoes beneath St. Peter's Basilica. The marble sarcophagus is one of several unearthed, representing burials let down through the flooring in past centuries. The brick façade of a Roman mausoleum can be glimpsed to the right of the sarcophagus.

2.   The roofless Caetennius
tomb, first to be found, after
clearing of the interior. The
niches were intended for urn
burials, a few of which were
found in place. Laid into the
floor, at center, is the oblong
grave-slab covering the body of
the Christian woman, Aemelia
Gorgonia.

2A.   Tomb of a second-
century Roman merchant,
Popilius Heracla, showing the
interior still clogged with
earth-fill. A reference in the inscription above the door proves
that Nero's "circus" or arena
once stood nearby.

3. Water accumulation beneath St. Peter's was a problem as far back as the fifth century. Here three of the Sampietrini, hampered by a knee-deep flood, excavate along the line of Roman tombs. In this case the trouble was eventually traced to a break in an ancient conduit.

4.   The narrow street running between the two rows of second-century Roman tombs beneath the basilica. As with the tombs' interiors, the street too was buried under many tons of earth-fill. The view is west, looking toward the area under the basilica's high altar.

5. The street between the tombs, looking east. In the distance the original earth-fill can be seen still in place. The wooden catwalks overhead were installed as the original Grotto flooring was removed.

6. Crudely sketched heads on the wall of the central niche in the Valerius tomb. The upper drawing represents Christ, the lower depicts Peter. Most of the lengthy inscription found below the Peter head is still hidden by earth.

7.   The Christ-Helios mosaic on the ceiling of the Julius tomb, with the light rays from behind the head suggesting a cross. Entry to the tomb was made through the now-sealed opening at the left.

8. Monsignor Ludwig Kaas in his office at the Vatican, shortly before his death in 1952. Through the window is seen the dome of St. Peter's.

8A. Fr. Engelbert Kirschbaum, a leading figure in Christian archaeology, was one of the four scholars who formed the first excavation team appointed by Pius XII.

They agreed, however, that the marble-lined repository pre-
dated Constantine's basilica. Perhaps it had once held the
venerated bones of some early pope or saint, some distinguished
figure who had, like Pope Pius XI so many centuries later, been
eager for burial as close as possible to Peter. For whatever
reason, the cavity had probably been emptied some time in the
early Middle Ages, as the presence of the Limoges coin strongly
implied. How the removal had been accomplished, they could
only guess, but they noted that the marble endpiece at the left-
hand side was caved inward. This suggested that entry had been
gained from that direction, very likely during some forgotten
tenth-century alteration. Wishing to spare the graffiti wall from
further harm, anxious to begin exploring beneath the shrine,
they now turned their attention to the workman who stood
ready with pick and shovel.

Measurements previously taken of the whole area had shown
that the thick graffiti wall occupied a position just off the shrine's
center line, to the north. On the far side of this wall, therefore,
and some feet belowground, should be the site of Peter's grave.
The plan was to dig down beside the wall and then go under the
foundations, which should run no deeper than three or four feet.
At length, the marble flooring was taken up and the workman's
pick was soon chunking lightly into the hard underlying soil to
loosen it for shoveling.

At a depth of eighteen inches, straight down, a simple slab
grave was encountered, holding a portion of a skeleton. When
the grave proved to be of the fourth century, the bones were removed and the slabs cleared away. Another foot down and the
foundations of the wall came into view. They were made of
plain brick with a waterproof outer layer, and they rested
directly atop another slab grave. To the excavators' delight, this
grave proved to be of the first century. Quickly they decided
they would go no deeper but would proceed to break through
the exposed foundations.

Crouching at the bottom of the wide, four-foot-deep pit, a
workman with hammer and chisel gently chipped away the
outer plaster, then loosened brick after brick, passing each brick

in turn up to his helper. Working slowly and with deliberate skill, by the end of the day the workman had pushed his way almost through to the other side of the two-foot thickness, fashioning a rough opening. Scraping away mortar, he worked a last brick out of place and saw nothing but darkness within.

Kirschbaum, who was wearing overalls, quickly scrambled down into the pit and aimed a flashlight. Because of his nervous excitement and the sudden yellow glare, for a moment his straining eyes swam out of focus. As his vision cleared he found himself peering into an irregular little chamber, about four feet on a side with an earthen floor. It appeared to be empty. After a moment's hesitation, he turned around, stretched out on his back, and with the workman's help slowly squirmed his head and shoulders through the opening.

Looking up, he saw that the narrow ceiling, high above his head, was formed of a rectangular slab of marble, on which an inscription was neatly cut. The words were all run together, but he was just able to make out a name, *Aelius Isidorus*. Along with the additional words, the name made it clear that the slab was not an original part of the grave. Apparently it had once served as the title inscription for some nearby tomb. In its center, cutting through the inscription, was a small, square hole. Kirschbaum shone his light into it and saw the bottom of a shaft lined with green porphyry—the same shaft, undoubtedly, whose top had been investigated fifty years before by Grisar.

Turning his head to the right, Kirschbaum was surprised to see that there was no east wall, only the side of another grave, the marble slab of which closed the chamber at a slant. Turning to the left, he saw the foundations of the red wall, with still another niche cut into it, though a much rougher one than the two above. On the north side of the chamber, the side by which he had entered, there was nothing but the reverse of the graffiti wall, its lower portion faced with grayish marble.

Using some effort, Kirschbaum managed to twist his shoulders round and was able to see the wall behind his head. At its bottom was a layer of ancient brick, above this was a wide strip of packed earth, and this in turn was surmounted by another layer

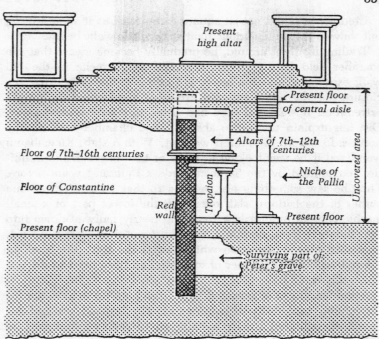

7. Side view beneath the high altar showing the relation of the red wall and the Tropaion to the remaining portion of Peter's grave. To the left is the present underground chapel, to the right is the open area.

of antique brickwork. These were the remnants of two low walls, he tentatively concluded, put up at different times. Though both remnants abutted on the red wall, it was evident that they had once extended farther. Most likely they had been cut off, shortened, when the red wall was erected. It was also apparent that they did not run at right angles to the red wall, as might have been expected. They slanted away markedly, at least ten degrees out of plumb. Looking up at the Isidorus slab, Kirschbaum noted something he had missed before. The slab was also twisted awry. It did not sit square to the wall as it should have, but showed the same curious slant as the little walls below.

Trailing his light around, he gradually became aware that the chamber held an air of disarray. The rough niche in the red wall, especially, and the heavy sill above it that supported the closure slab, had both suffered extensive breakage at their right extremities. It was as if they had been purposely hacked away. Did this explain the entire absence of a chamber wall on the north side, where the graffiti wall sat? With a sigh, Kirschbaum wondered if he was looking at some of the "unspeakable iniquities" committed by the Saracen horde a thousand years before. Then he saw something else, adding to that impression. At one corner of the Isidorus slab overhead, the lower part of a small marble column hung askew, reaching nearly halfway down into the chamber. Here, certainly, was the twin of the left-hand column seen aboveground, on which rested the travertine shelf in the red wall. What manner of violence had been used to drive it down this way?

A sudden gleam of reflected light from high up behind the little column caught Kirschbaum's eye. He reached up and his fingers encountered a sharp metallic edge. Taking a firm grip, he pulled. Down on his face came a fine shower of mortar, but in his hand he held a thin, rectangular plate of gold, measuring about two by three inches. Embossed on its shining surface was a pair of open eyes, and between them a cross. Kirschbaum had seen such objects before and he recognized the plate as a votive offering, almost certainly given for the healing of an eye. He judged that it could be as early as the fifth or sixth century. After a moment's study he passed the plate out to the waiting workman for the others to see.

Now his light picked out, lying here and there on ledges and projections, a scattering of coins, most of them darkened with age. Under his head and back, he suddenly realized, many more coins littered the chamber floor. Picking up a few, he held them to the light but was unable to read any of the inscriptions. Some contained the heads of what appeared to be Roman emperors.

As the light continued slowly to search into cracks and crevasses, Kirschbaum spotted another feature he had missed. At the bottom of the niche in the red wall foundations, where they disappeared into the dirt floor, there was a small opening. He inserted an exploratory hand but felt nothing. Then he scraped away some of the dirt. The space was not just an opening, it was a large gap in the structure of the wall itself, shaped like an inverted V, apparently a rise and fall in the foundations.

Running his hand over the dirt that almost filled the gap, he felt his fingers brush something hard embedded in the earth. He scraped around the object, then gently pulled it free. Holding it up, he saw that it was a bone, about five inches long. He turned it around and over, finally deciding that it might easily be from a human arm or leg—momentarily his hand trembled at the thought that he could be holding a part of the body of St. Peter. Rolling over on his side, he aimed his flashlight under the wall. More bones, deeply embedded, were piled in and around the same spot. Carefully, he replaced the bone, then called to be pulled out of the chamber. Within seconds he was excitedly reporting his find to the others.

It was now evening, not far from the basilica's closing time, but one of the excavators immediately hurried off to inform Pius XII of the discovery. At the same time, workmen were sent to procure some of the special lead-lined boxes that had been prepared for holding any random bones turned up in the digging.

Within ten minutes, the white-cassocked Pope arrived on the scene, his sharp intellectual features drawn, the piercing eyes alert behind the round glasses. Kirschbaum explained the situation to him, pointing out that the bones did not lie spread along the surface but were more or less all heaped together, without covering or protection, about a foot down in the bare earth. Little could be done with them, he said, while they lay in so difficult a position.

Some sober discussion among the Pope and the four archaeologists followed, and at length the Pope gave permission for the

bones to be unearthed. A chair was placed on the marble pavement just above the pit and the Pope sat down. Kirschbaum,
armed with a trowel and brush, squirmed his way back into the
chamber.

During the next several hours, bone after bone was gingerly
passed out, some broken or reduced by decay, many more only
fragments, and all were carefully deposited in the boxes at the
Pope's feet. Most were small, many even tiny, representing various vertebrae, parts of fingers and toes, and parts of shattered
ribs, as well as some bits and pieces that were not immediately
identifiable. A good many were large, however, and apparently
intact, and though none of the excavators had any real medical
knowledge, it seemed certain that whole bones, or nearly whole,
were present from both the arms and the legs. There was also a
large segment of the breastbone, and part of a shoulder blade.

At the finish, a total of at least 250 pieces, large and small, had
been extracted. To the onlookers, gazing in wonder at the three
boxes, each holding in its bottom a single layer of bones, it appeared that there must be almost enough to make an entire skeleton.

The one part of the body which all were waiting to see was
the skull, but this did not appear, nor could any of the fragments
be identified as belonging to it. Far from feeling disappointment,
however, the Pope and the others regarded this absence of a
skull as a singularly positive sign. Among the many precious
relics preserved in the numerous churches of Rome, one of the
most precious was claimed to be precisely the head of Peter.
Since at least the ninth century it had lain in a reliquary above
the altar in the Cathedral of St. John Lateran. No one could
guarantee its authenticity, no one knew exactly where it had
come from, or how it had reached the Lateran (speculation
suggested an effort to save it from the barbarian invaders who
twice sacked Rome in the fourth century, though the danger
might equally have come from the Saracens). But the mere fact
of the claim now assumed some relevance.

The absence of a skull among the bones beneath the shrine,

and the presence of a head in the Lateran, accepted for a millennium as Peter's, were points dovetailing too neatly to be ignored. Only once in modern times had the Lateran reliquary been opened, in 1804, and that inspection had confirmed at least the nature of the contents. Still remaining were a portion of the cranium, a part of the jawbone with some teeth, a few vertebrae, and much dust.

The feeling that this strange cache of bones from under the red wall comprised the earthly remains of St. Peter—the first pope, the Rock on whom the church was founded, the man who in the Gospels walks so humanly at the right hand of Jesus—took strong hold of all those connected with the excavation, including Pius XII. Yet even in their mood of quiet exultation none went so far as to voice anything like certainty. The circumstances were simply too vague for that, and nothing additional had been found under the red wall to aid identification.

All that could be concluded, and then only as probable, was that at some unknown time, for obscure reasons, the bones had been deliberately piled together and pushed below the triangular rise in the foundations. It was an act that might or might not have been connected with the Saracen threat, or with some other less well remembered time of danger. In any case, they were human bones and they had been found in what was unquestionably Peter's own grave. They had definitely lain there untouched for at least a thousand years. In the absence of contrary evidence, it was easy to believe that they had been in the grave, reverently tended as it had always been, from the very start.

Expressing his gratitude to the four archaeologists, and the Sampietrini, the Pope directed that the lead boxes be locked and sealed, and taken to his private apartment in the Vatican. There, during the ensuing months, a minute examination was performed on the bones by the Pope's personal physician, Dr. Galeazzi-Lisi, and several medical experts. Their report to the Pope stated that, without doubt, the bones were those of a man, powerfully built, who had been perhaps sixty-five or seventy years old at death. These facts fitted well with the tradition regarding Peter. Beyond that, nothing could be said.

No word of this discovery had yet reached the public, nor would it for eight more years. The public, in any case, might not at that time have stopped to listen. World War II had erupted in earnest.

5

The Red Wall Complex

As excavation continued during the next three years in the area surrounding the shrine, the full history of Peter's grave steadily unrolled itself, enabling the excavators to piece together a remarkable record of devotion to the apostle's memory. Inevitably, as work progressed the operations became increasingly more difficult and delicate, requiring an ever slower and more painstaking approach. Often it became necessary, in order to avoid inflicting irreparable damage, for the workmen to burrow horizontally through the soil, rather than digging straight down through the floors, an approach that called for a good deal of patient shoring up. The small team of scientists kept faithfully at its task, however, and though these were the war years the internal affairs of Vatican City remained largely free of serious disruption. "The passions and varying fortunes of war," Monsignor Kaas later recalled, "scarcely disturbed the labors in the secluded and hallowed earth."

First to be investigated was the earthen floor of the central chamber, now tacitly accepted as Peter's grave, though admittedly it was not in its original condition. The level of the chamber floor was taken down about three feet, the soil being passed out to workmen who put it through a sifter. While nothing further bearing directly on the question of Peter's body was found, each trowelful of earth did yield many coins, all dulled and blackened, most in a state of at least partial corrosion. Together with the stray coins recovered from aboveground in the chamber, and at various levels higher up, the total collected came to nearly two thousand.

Immediately, specialists began a study of this hoard and, as expected, the dates of most of the coins were found to coincide with the whole period of Constantine's basilica, the fourth to fifteenth centuries. They came from almost every country of Europe, with Italy, France, and Germany predominating. Most significant was a batch of over forty from Imperial Rome, both bronze and silver, which proved to have been minted well before Constantine, in the first to third centuries (this total might have been much higher, but more than half of the eight hundred Roman coins found were far too corroded for precise recognition).

The earliest coin was a bronze from the time of Augustus, minted at the latest by A.D. 14. There were two other coins from the first century, and four from the second. Since it was unlikely that coins would still be in circulation even fifty years after minting, these earlier coins were taken as evidence of a steady devotion to Peter's memory during that long and obscure period stretching backward from Constantine to the decade of Peter's burial. The presence of early coins in the central chamber, the grave itself, seemed proof positive that a way had been left open, perhaps from the very start, to permit some sort of contact with the body.

Of even greater significance than the coins was the unraveling of the complex of other structures that lay around the shrine. Most of the elements in immediate contact with the red wall, it was found, bore a definite and close structural relationship, confronting the archaeologists with an unexpected challenge. In the end they succeeded in putting together an intriguing picture.

The red wall when first built had indeed been longer, stretching for no less than twenty-six feet, an additional ten feet or so on either side of the remaining portion. At its southern end it had met the rear wall of another pagan mausoleum—of this only

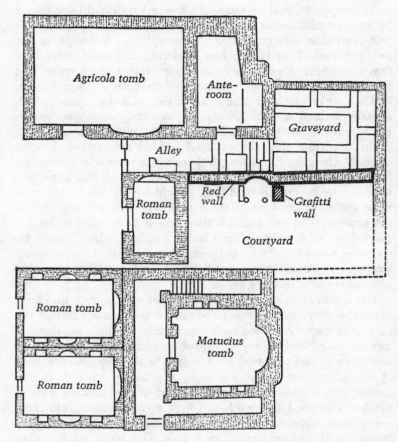

8. Plan of the second-century red wall complex uncovered beneath the basilica's high altar, with adjacent Roman tombs.

the foundations had been preserved—standing next in line to the Matucius tomb.

At its opposite end, to the north, the red wall had been joined by another wall, set at a right angle, suggesting an enclosure. It was clear that a large rectangular area, equal in length to the red wall and about twelve feet in depth, had once stood here free and unoccupied. The entire floor of this open space had been covered by a paving of tiles, white with a green border, laid in part on earth-fill. The focus of this walled-in space, which actually formed a small courtyard, was the two-niched monument built into the red wall, heavy with its travertine shelf.

On its reverse side, the red wall yielded discoveries of equal interest. Along its entire length there ran a narrow alleyway, six feet wide with a concrete floor. The far side of this alley was bounded by two small buildings, of which only the lower walls were still in place. One of these buildings was a tomb, and to the excavators' surprise and satisfaction it was found to be the mausoleum of the outspoken Flavius Agricola, whose pagan inscription had so upset its sixteenth-century discoverers. Heavily wrapped, Agricola's remains still lay in the large lidless sarcophagus, along with those of his wife.

The Agricola tomb was the outermost of the two buildings along the alleyway, the first to be passed by anyone entering the narrow passage. Attached to its rear wall was the second structure, a tomb-like building of uncertain purpose. There were no burials in it, and no provision for any. Sunk deep into the floor at one corner was a large cistern, a puzzling feature. In the earlier excavations under the main part of the basilica, two of the larger tombs had been found with such anterooms attached, one with a cistern. But those anterooms stood at the tombs' fronts and served as normal courtyards. This room, on the other hand, was attached at the back of its companion, and its only door opened directly into the alley. Between the two there was no interior passage, no access of any kind. Despite these anomalies, the team concluded that the second building still must have been an anteroom, a waiting or resting chamber for visitors to the Agricola mausoleum. Perhaps the lay of the land had dictated its peculiar position.

The alleyway itself, at its entrance, had been closed by a heavy ironwork door set in a fine travertine frame. At its farther end, a short flight of steps—rising just behind the monument in the red wall—led up to another burial area, the most distinctive in the whole cemetery. It was not an enclosed tomb but another open courtyard, almost square, surrounded by thick walls, one of which was the northern extension of the red wall. The floor was paved with tile, and underneath, ranged around the perimeter, were spaces for at least six coffins. None of these spaces contained a burial, a curious fact which did not seem a bar to the excavators' conclusion: here was the second-century "burial ground for bishops" which the old documents located adjacent to Peter's grave. The bodies which must once have lain here perhaps had been removed at the building of Constantine's basilica. In any case, there was no provision for cremation burial in this unique open-air mausoleum, and that fact was sufficient to establish it as Christian.

It was only with much difficulty that the diggers were able to extend their probe even a short way beneath the white-tiled courtyard that lay spread in front of the red wall. Their persistence brought its reward when they succeeded in finding at least seven graves, of a simpler type, dating to the late first and early second centuries. Revealingly, all seven lay crowded close round that of Peter. There could be no doubt that they had been carefully placed and angled, even crossing and lying atop one another, in order to be as near as possible to the apostle's body.

In one of the seven, as Kirschbaum reported, the corpse had "dwindled to a few centimeters of brownish-yellow remains, with here and there the gleam of golden threads, which let us form our conclusions as to the precious garments of the dead man and his social status." Here was the body of an early pope, the archaeologists felt sure, probably one of the ten who had reigned after Peter up to the mid-second century (all of whom had also been martyred). Two of the graves, the earliest and the nearest to Peter, showed that same misalignment noted by Kirschbaum as he lay in the chamber (now computed to be exactly eleven degrees from the right angle).

Of supreme importance for the entire operation was the question of dating. In the early fourth century Constantine had found this red wall complex standing, and had enshrined it. But how long had it stood on Vatican Hill before that, just how far back did it go? In order to identify the monument in the red wall as the Tropaion of Gaius, clear proof was needed that it had been in existence by the year 200, well over a century before Constantine.

By close analysis of building techniques and structural links, the excavators had already established that all the elements of this central area—the red wall with its niched monument and open courtyard, the alleyway and the open graveyard to which it led—had been built roughly at the same time, certainly within several years of each other. If any one of these elements could be dated, then all would fall into place. In the latter stages of the work, the hope of uncovering some clue to age had been uppermost.

The break came when a workman digging beneath the alleyway reported that a drainage ditch lay hidden under the concrete. Extending all the way from the upper burial ground to the alley's entrance door and beyond, the narrow ditch was lined and covered with long, flat tiles. When one of these was exposed to view, its underside showed an embossed symbol, a circular stamp serving as a manufacturer's mark. Quite legible, it soon yielded its meaning.

The tile had come from a brickworks owned by the Emperor Marcus Aurelius and his wife Faustina. On the stamp Marcus Aurelius was named as *Caesar*, showing that he had not at that time been proclaimed sole emperor, and Faustina was given the title *Augusta*. Exact dates for the events connected with these titles were available in Roman history: Faustina was designated *Augusta* in A.D. 147, and it was in 161, following the death of the Emperor Antoninus Pius, that her husband was elevated from *Caesar* to the imperial purple. When four additional tiles were found bearing the same seal, the excavators had their certainty. With full conviction, they concluded that the whole red wall complex had been built after the year 147, but not later than about 165, allowing ample time for tiles already in stock to be used up.

This welcome dating quickly led the four to make a speculative jump, spanning the decades back to the apostle's burial.

If the monument had been built in the earlier part of the period, say about 150, then Peter would have been in his grave scarcely eighty years at the time. Even at the outside, the interval between Peter's death and the building of the red wall would have covered hardly a century. The implications were obvious: among the first visitors to the new monument must have been some sons and daughters, certainly some of the grandchildren or other descendants, of those Roman Christians who had actually watched Peter being led to crucifixion, who had stood witness as his wracked and lifeless body was lowered into the earth. These first visitors, possessing a very recent and personal tradition about Peter, could hardly have been misled as to the location of his grave. And since the Tropaion had certainly been built by the official church of the period, the pope and his ministers, immediate inheritors of all that had occurred under the bloodthirsty Nero, these too would have had living, word-of-mouth memories of the martyred first pope, and the true location of his grave.

There was one final point, adding to the team's certainty about the Tropaion, and helping to fix the date of its construction more exactly. The old document known as the *Liber Pontificalis* (*Book of the Popes*, containing material as old as the sixth century) stated that it was Pope Anacletus, near the close of the first century, who had "built and set in order a memorial shrine to the blessed Peter where the bishops might be buried." No trace of a first-century shrine had been uncovered, yet the description did seem to fit the red wall complex, now known to have been erected some sixty or seventy years after Anacletus. During the period 155–66 the chair of Peter had been occupied by a man who bore a name very similar to the earlier pope: Anicetus. It would not be at all surprising, the excavators felt, if the scribe who worked on the *Liber Pontificalis* had mixed up names that were so close in both time and appearance.

9. Sketch reconstruction of the alleyway running behind the red wall (right). On the left is the low entrance to the curious anteroom. Through the upper door is the tile-floored burial ground. (See photographs 18, 19.)

While it was now certain that the 1,800-year-old Tropaion stood within the shrine—at least its main elements—the unusual design presented the archaeologists with something of an enigma. Nothing quite like this Tropaion had previously been found from Christian antiquity, and nothing about it, so far as could be seen or deduced, was expressly Christian. Its two niches (a broad upper one with a window-like aperture cut through it, and a lower, narrower one, the two niches separated by a jutting, table-like shelf) could be duplicated only in pagan funerary architecture, and even there only approximately. In several cemeteries of pagan Rome similar structures, though much smaller, had occasionally been found built up against walls. But these were intended to hold urns for cremation burials, not to mark earth-graves. They had box-like lower portions, not open niches flanked by columns supporting a semi-table, and were usually adorned with statuary and inscribed tablets.

The Tropaion, on the other hand, stood double the height of these pagan monuments—its original top must have reached well above ten feet—was proportionately wider, and must have been crowned by some sort of gable, perhaps the usual triangular pediment. In any case, this probable derivation from pagan designs was the best the excavators could do in explaining the Tropaion. What exact purpose the two niches might have served, especially the upper one with its curious aperture, why there should be a niche underground, why in the first place the second-century church should have chosen this unique form for Peter's monument, were questions they had to leave unresolved.

Before Constantine enclosed the Tropaion in his basilica it had been in place on the red wall for at least a hundred and fifty years, though it could well have been nearer two hundred. During that period, four or five generations of Christians had lived and died, many as martyrs in the spasmodic persecutions that broke out in Rome and across the Empire. Whether in its earlier years the Tropaion had served these generations as a center of devotion could not be determined. But the graffiti wall beside it, with its numerous inscriptions, supplied abundant proof that at least later the site had been a focus for pilgrims.

The graffiti wall, as suspected, was not an integral or original part of the complex. It was really an effort, rather clumsy, to repair damage which at one point had threatened the stability of the red wall and the Tropaion itself. About the mid third century, after the wall had been standing some hundred years, it developed a serious vertical crack, extending from top to bottom and running through the brickwork from front to back, probably as a result of settling. This fault, located only a few inches to the right of the Tropaion, had presented a major problem, one difficult to solve without endangering the monument. Finally, the thick graffiti wall was erected as a buttress, one end of it standing against the red wall and covering the crack.

To position the buttress properly the builders had been forced to encroach on the Tropaion, shortening the right edge of the shelf, and shifting its support column a little in toward the center. This move had impaired the Tropaion's symmetry, and over the next few years attempts were made to correct the defect, mostly by putting up small matching walls and lavishing marble all round the lower niche. Nothing could quite hide the disproportion, however, nor did Constantine's architects a century later make any attempt of their own at correction. After slicing off the outer ends of the red wall, they simply enclosed everything in the marble housing. Why they chose to leave the bulky graffiti wall in place when they might easily have dispensed with it, restoring the monument's symmetry, was uncertain. Perhaps, thought the excavators, the wall with its precious freight of inscriptions was by Constantine's day simply accepted as a permanent part of the monument (today the asymmetry is still visible when viewed from the Niche of the Pallia).

The picture of Peter's primitive grave, in the years before the Tropaion, had also become sufficiently clear. The burial itself must have been unobtrusive, even hurried, since the Roman authorities would hardly have permitted a public ceremony for an executed Christian, even if Peter's followers had cared to chance it. For the same reason the grave, not far from the place of execution, would almost certainly have been an ordinary one, sunk in the earth, with Peter's body perhaps resting in a coffin, perhaps protected only by the usual slabs of tile (this did not rule out the problematic Senator Marcellus, who might, for instance, have owned the plot of ground). Twice in the following decades low walls were put up around the grave, both to mark it and to protect it from the rising earth on the hillside, a result of the building of tombs nearby.

When it came time to build the Tropaion a century or so after the burial, the orientation of the red wall had to conform to the line and arrangement of the imposing pagan mausoleums now hedging closely round the site. This had forced the red wall to cut directly across Peter's grave almost at its center, and at a decided angle. It may have been now that the grave was shortened, rather than later, but in any case, it was evident that the builders had taken great care to preserve as much of it as they could, including its alignment on the hillside. They lifted the red wall foundations over the grave in an inverted V, and left standing a remnant of the two low brick walls in their angled position. The closure slab atop the chamber was also preserved intact, twisting away from the red wall at the same eleven degrees. The whole careful operation bespoke a strong desire not to lose sight of the primitive grave, while fitting the new monument into the surrounding pattern of tombs.

At the shortening of the grave Peter's remains, by then perhaps only bones, must have been collected together in the surviving portion. From this it could fairly be said that the cache of bones found buried under the red wall, though not in the central chamber, still lay in what had once been Peter's own grave, the filled-in half. This did not answer the nagging question of how they had gotten there, though the Saracen threat seemed a sufficient reason for the removal. At the approach of the invaders, the bones had been taken out of the receptacle—whether or not a bronze coffin—and since the pious attitudes of the time would not allow them to be altogether separated from their original resting place, they had been reburied under the red wall, no doubt with the intention of restoring them to the central chamber when the danger had passed. As the centuries rolled on, they had simply been permitted to remain under the wall.

Aside from the question of the bones, so far as the excavators were concerned the continuity of Peter's grave, from the moment of burial until the broaching of the central chamber twenty centuries later, was now complete and indisputable. The ancient tradition had been tested, and had held. It was while pondering this marvel of history, for which there existed no real parallel, that Kirschbaum was moved to offer a final comment:

Normally, graves have no history, not even the history of their development . . . their zenith is at their start. What comes after is disintegration. This is true not only of the modest graves of ordinary mortals, which barely last for two or three generations, it is true also of the world's proudest funerary monuments, the royal pyramids of Egypt or the gigantic mausoleums of ancient Rome. True, they have endured for thousands of years, but in gradual decay. All that remains is a dreadful shadow of their onetime magnificence.

Few graves on earth have transcended this interior rhythm of death and disintegration. And these are not the tombs of the mighty ones of earth, but those of the saints, who even after their deaths live on in the world with a mysterious effectiveness—among them, this apostolic grave with its remarkable and mysterious power, and an influence that develops through the centuries.

6

Stroke of Fate

By the close of 1945, work at the shrine was virtually complete, and preparation of a full report was under way. Planned to fill two oversize volumes, detailing and illustrating every step of the work beneath the high altar, with many photographs and drawings and a lengthy text, the labor of compilation and writing would be formidable, delaying publication for several years. Since the Pope had already designated 1950 as a Holy Year, it was decided that appearance of the report during that time of special observance would be most fitting. The first official announcement to the world would be made personally by Pius XII on the day before Christmas, 1949. Meantime, even though rumors were already circulating, no information was to be given out.

It was an enterprising Italian journalist with Vatican connections, Camille Gianfara, who short-circuited these careful plans, managing in the process to misplace the emphasis. On August 22, 1949, his story, centering on the relics, made front-page headlines around the world. Except for a passing reference to one of the excavators, Enrico Josi, the sources were carefully concealed. In a page-one headline the New York *Times* declared:

BONES OF ST. PETER FOUND
UNDER ALTAR, VATICAN BELIEVES
Reported to be in an urn guarded by Pontiff;
neutral experts will be asked to
check discovery under basilica

The bones had been found, said the account, in a "subterranean cell" about twenty feet down beneath the high altar, where they had lain in a "terracotta urn." All those concerned in the project, the *Times* explained, had for the time being been sworn to secrecy.

Technical and other problems delayed the printing of the report and it was not until over a year later that the Pope, speaking by radio, made the news official, at the same time taking care to correct the emphasis.

"Has the tomb of St. Peter really been found?" he asked. "To that question the answer is beyond all doubt, *yes*. The tomb of the Prince of the Apostles has been found. Such is the final conclusion after all the labor and study of these years. A second question, subordinate to the first, refers to the relics of St. Peter. Have they been found? At the side of the tomb remains of human bones have been discovered. However, it is impossible to prove with certainty that they belong to the body of the apostle. This still leaves intact the historical reality of the tomb itself."

The Pope's reserve in the matter of the bones was strictly accurate. Still, though many wondered what was meant by the phrase "at the side of the tomb," the belief quickly gained ground that these mysterious bones *must* be those of the apostle. In the total absence of any evidence to the contrary, such a conclusion on the public's part was almost inevitable. When the report finally appeared some months later—two huge, expensive volumes intended for the world's libraries—it contained a photograph of several of the larger bones lying at the edge of the V-shaped opening under the red wall. Special permission had been obtained to replace them for the picture. The accompanying text, in an effort to be scrupulously objective, stated only that "some human bones" had been found mingled in the earth beneath the wall. There was no effort to describe the bones, no explanation of what studies had been performed on them, and no attempt to relate them to Peter.

The Pope's conviction about the tomb's authenticity was based, as he said, on all the labor and study of the previous decade. But he had also received, almost at the last moment, word of another discovery, much belated, which had provided the final link in the chain of evidence. Sometime in early December 1950, too late for inclusion in the report, the name of Peter had at last been found in connection with the Tropaion.

One of the excavators, Antonio Ferrua, still curious about the marble repository in the graffiti wall, had been canvassing the area one day when, for no particular reason, he stooped and shone his light into the opening. Lying on the bottom in the right corner was a small chunk of masonry, which certainly had not been there even a few days before. Ferrua reached in and took it out, noticing in some surprise that it was a piece of plaster from the red wall. Somehow it had been jarred loose from its position immediately above the marble end-slab, and had fallen intact.

Seen close up, the red plaster was rather rough and somewhat pitted, and at first Ferrua noticed nothing unusual.

Then as the light fell at just the right angle, there leaped out at him two lines of scratched letters, all about two inches high: ΠΕΤΡ . . . , and below it, ΕΝΙ . . . The plaster was broken off at the termination of both these words, but it required only a few seconds for Ferrua to see that the first was Peter's name in Greek, ΠΕΤΡΟΣ (*Petros*). The second line, incomplete as it was, presented more difficulty. Perhaps it was an invocation for prayers to the apostle, a point which could be settled only by the missing letters. At any rate, the second word hardly mattered. Here, beyond cavil, was Peter's name at last, scratched on the wall above and just to the right of his grave.

Obviously, the inscription had been written on the red wall prior to the erection of the graffiti wall in front of it. That fact, and its use of Greek, which by the late third century had almost

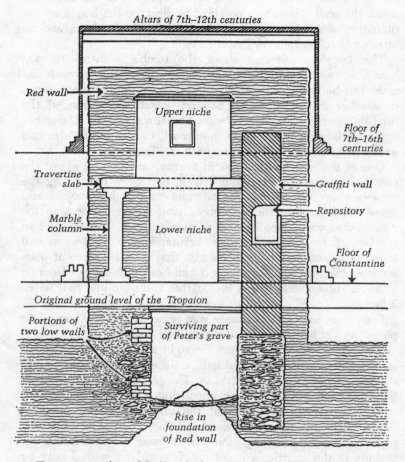

10. Front view (simplified) of the red wall with its niches, the Tropaion, and the graffiti wall, in relation to the underground portions of the monument and Peter's grave.

9. Sketch reconstruction of the original shrine erected by the Emperor
Constantine about A.D. 320 in the first basilica, to honor and preserve
Peter's grave. A portion of the marble housing at the center was found by
the modern excavators still in place.

9A. A later remodeling (seventh century) of the original Constantinian
shrine and the high altar area. The marble shrine, here located directly
under the main altar, is hidden from view by the broad, high platform. The
unique twisted columns, their positions shifted, are the same that flanked
the first arrangement.

10. The present high altar of St. Peter's, showing the sunken area (*Confessio*) with its heavy doors closed upon the Niche of the Pallia. On the other side of the altar, opposite the Niche, is the underground chapel where the excavations began. The unusual design of the area was an effort to preserve some access to the shrine over Peter's grave.

11. The Niche of the Pallia where by tradition a new bishop's *pallium* or stole rests overnight before being bestowed. Note the lopsided design, a structural puzzle which was solved only during the excavations.

12.   The front wall of the underground chapel, after dismantling. Visible at
center is the marble wall of Constantine's fourth-century shrine, with a
strip of porphyry running down its middle. Above it is the twelfth-century
altar of Pope Calixtus II.

13. The north side of the shrine beneath the high altar, after breaching by the excavators. One of the small marble columns that supported the second-century Tropaion can be seen, still in its original position.

14. The second-century graffiti wall (inner surface) discovered on the south side of the shrine. Part of the rough opening into the hidden repository is just visible at the right. The outer walls date to the Middle Ages. Between, stood another brick-and-mortar wall of the fourth century, here removed.

15.   The central chamber in the original soil of Vatican Hill deep beneath the high altar, identified as the remaining portion of Peter's grave. Remnants of two low walls, one atop the other and separated by a layer of earth, can be seen at the far side. Both abut (right) on the rim of the underground niche in the red wall's foundation.

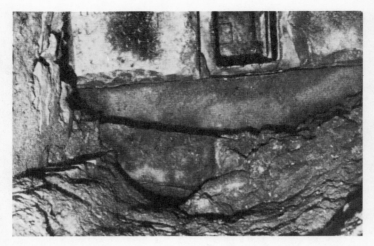

16.   The ceiling of the central chamber, Peter's grave, showing the overhead closure slab and its peculiar out-of-plumb angling. This feature of the construction preserves the original grave's true orientation on the hillside.

16A.   Some of the human bones found in the earth beneath the triangular rise of the red wall foundation in Peter's grave. After excavation, these few bones were replaced atop the soil for the photograph.

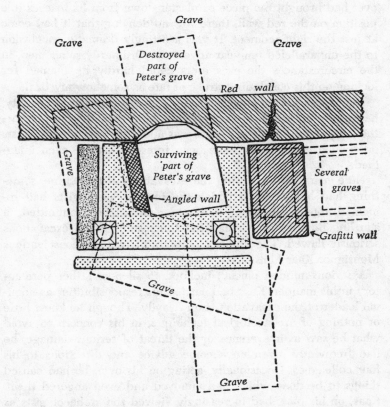

11. Overhead view of Peter's original grave showing its angled position in relation to the red wall, and some of the surrounding first- and second-century burials.

disappeared from Roman usage, made a date as early as A.D. 200 not unreasonable. This was almost too eerie a denouement, and as the four excavators eagerly examined the unmistakable scratches, they could only shake their heads in wonder. What ever had brought the piece of plaster down from its inaccessible position on the red wall, there was no denying that it had come at just the right moment. It was a fittingly dramatic conclusion to the unparalleled ten-year adventure. Ordinarily sober men, in the circumstances the excavators could hardly be blamed for looking on this concluding stroke of fate as somehow mystical.

But it was not a conclusion, mystical or otherwise. In reality, because of an earlier act of fate, less kind than the closing one, the long search for Peter's relics was about to enter a new phase, one which could never have been foreseen, hardly even imagined.

Nine years before, during the excavations at the shrine, something had happened of which the four archaeologists had remained totally unaware. A blunder had been committed, a startling blunder, which had left the results of the excavations seriously flawed. The unlucky perpetrator was the conscientious Monsignor Kaas himself.

A serious-minded official, inclined to silence, rather peremptory in his manner, Kaas had carried his responsibilities as nominal leader of the excavation team heavily. Though he knew little or nothing of archaeological technique, in his concern to avoid what he saw as irreverence or the threat of serious damage, he had frequently given unwelcome advice and directions to his four colleagues. Occasionally, acting on his own, he had caused things to be done which had annoyed and even angered them. Kaas, on his part, had increasingly viewed the archaeologists as too blunt and casual in their methods, even insensitive.

Perhaps inevitably, the operations under the basilica had not been many months old when the breach widened, and soon nearly all direct contact between Kaas and the team had ceased. They seldom met and when they did they were never more than polite, with only necessary matters being discussed. It was this lamentable atmosphere, unguessed by outsiders at the time, which had made the blunder possible.

It was Kaas' practice late each evening, after everyone had departed and the excavations lay quiet, lit dimly here and there by night lights, to tour the whole area accompanied by one of the foremen of the Sampietrini, Giovanni Segoni. Almost never present during the day's work, on these daily tours Kaas would inspect every detail of the most recent digging and dismantling. As the work beneath the body of the basilica brought to light stray parts of skeletons, he had made it his personal duty to see that no human bones should, in the confusion of cleaning up, become mixed with the mounds of dirt and debris and be accidentally thrown out. Whenever bones were found, including an occasional skull, he had them placed in special boxes and stored away for reburial. The other four knew of Kaas' inspection routine and grudgingly accepted it, though they were seldom informed of its daily results.

One evening early in 1942, a day or so after the team had first exposed the graffiti wall and peered briefly into the man-made cavity, intending to return later for a closer look, Kaas had come to the area on his rounds, along with the foreman. Segoni, flaking off some of the plaster rim for a better view, inspected the cavity with a light. When he reported what appeared to be a number of bones mixed with some debris, Kaas unhesitatingly told him to remove them for safekeeping.

Breaking off a few further bits of plaster from the hole's edge, no more than was necessary, Segoni began handing out the contents. Besides lumps of mortar and brick which had fallen down from the wall-fill above, there were many human bones, all bleached to a stark whiteness. Reverently, Kaas placed them one by one in a box. Segoni then swept his hand over the bottom slab, as far as he could reach through the small aperture. Along with gravel and bits of plaster, he picked up some more fragments of bone, some shreds of cloth, a few thick threads, and two corroded coins. These things he also placed in the box. Then, at Kaas' direction, he wrote out a label on a small card: "*ossa—urna—graf*" (bones, graffiti urn).

Several days later the four archaeologists, after completing their disappointing investigation of the Pallia Niche, returned to the graffiti wall. Intent on the exciting culmination of their search, an entry into the central chamber, they never noticed that the opening into the cavity had in the meantime been slightly enlarged. Making their own inspection of the curious repository, they found only the bits of debris that Segoni's probing hand had missed: some threads, the bits of metal, the Limoges coin, and the few chips of bone.

7

The Wooden Box

It was like walking down a narrow, deserted side street in old Rome, some silent midnight, when the mingled voices and the hurrying tread of many sandals had all faded away, the inhabitants sunk at last to blessed sleep. Nestled under the wide-spreading mantle of the basilica's marble floor, a tiny portion of the ancient city had emerged ghost-like from its interminable sepulture.

Each of the nineteen tombs beneath the body of the basilica had now been cleared, inside and out, of its clogging deposit of earth. Running between the two rows, the little street lay open all the way to the area beneath the high altar, where it wound into the alley behind the red wall. Along the right side of the street there stretched an even row of handsome brick façades, rising trimly to varying heights of twelve or fifteen feet, their ragged tops lost in shadow. Opposite, along the left, there ran the rear walls of the second row, the reddish brickwork with the interstices picked out in white looking remarkably fresh after sixteen centuries in the earth.

Though somewhat damaged here and there, many of the neat façades on the right still supported tasteful terracotta figurines and marble nameplates. The open doorways, all of them framed by slabs of travertine, allowed elongated patches of murky light from newly installed electric bulbs to drape at intervals across the street. It was the spring of 1952 and this rediscovered Roman city of the dead was being readied to stand on permanent exhibition.

Requests to visit the site had flooded in, from professional and amateur archaeologists, classical scholars, historians, journalists, students, and the curious, but very few outsiders had as yet gained entry. As so often with archaeologists, from the start the excavators had jealously guarded their treasure, strictly excluding even professional visitors until the final urn had been identified, the last brick measured.

Those who did manage to obtain special consideration had all come on urgent scientific errands, eager to see and study some particular rarity. Among the first of the early visitors (granted the privilege by Pius XII himself) was a member of the faculty of the University of Rome, a professor of Greek epigraphy, Dr. Margherita Guarducci. She arrived on the scene in May 1952, anxious to study the tantalizing, still only partially deciphered Peter graffito in the Valerius tomb.

Just fifty years old, Dr. Guarducci brought with her a background of experience that few could equal. The many thousands of hours she had spent peering at ancient epigraphs of all sorts —words incised on worn marble or scratched on stone now crumbling, epitaphs chiseled on moldering graves and monuments, mottoes embossed on medals, plate, old coins, and every other sort of durable material—had marvelously sharpened both her searching eye and her intuitive perception. Especially in the arduous task of unraveling graffiti of a more haphazard kind, doubly alien to modern eyes in its cursive nature and heedless execution, she could frequently almost discern the personality behind the dead hand that had made it. Unmarried, for nearly thirty years she had poured all her energies into scholarship, becoming deeply learned in the ancient Greek and Roman civilizations. More than 140 articles in scholarly journals bore her name, and her multi-volume collection of inscriptions from ancient Crete had already taken its place as a standard sourcebook. Finely attuned to all that related to Rome and its turbulent history, perhaps no better-equipped, no more-industrious scholar could have been found for the work which—at this moment unknown to all—still waited to be done.

Accompanying Dr. Guarducci on her first trip to the necropolis was Monsignor Francesco Vacchini, chief engineer of St. Peter's Basilica. Some months before, Monsignor Kaas, then in his seventies, had fallen ill and shortly afterward had died. Until a new adminstrator could be named, Vacchini was filling in.

Entering the narrow street of the necropolis, the two strolled past the first seven tombs, pausing only long enough at each door for a brief look inside. At the Valerius mausoleum they turned into the small outer courtyard, with its wall niches containing marble funerary urns, then stepped over the high stone threshold into the main part of the tomb. Distracted for a moment by the marvelous display of stucco statuary, Dr. Guarducci's gaze soon eagerly focused on the central niche, just opposite the door. From fifteen feet away, the sketched heads and the inscription were barely visible. It was only on approaching closer that, in some dismay, she realized the truth.

For a decade now these wall markings had stood uncovered, in conditions that were frequently very humid because of the Vatican's notorious water seepage problem. This was a situation she had not foreseen. During those ten crucial years since the discovery, a gradual but steady fading of both the charcoal and the red lead had continued, with the result that at many points portions of the scrawled lines had simply disappeared. Her task, she concluded with a regretful sigh for the wasted years, was to be much more difficult than she had imagined.

Before setting to work, with Monsignor Vacchini she completed a tour of the necropolis, coming finally to the jumble of names crowded onto the surface of the graffiti wall beside Peter's grave. This feature of the excavations had been described in the official report, very briefly, as a highly interesting but essentially straightforward collection of names and prayers, of the sort often found at venerated graves in antiquity. There had been no sign that anything more unusual was present, and lacking, as it apparently did, any real challenge for an expert, the

wall had failed to arouse in Dr. Guarducci more than a mild curiosity. Now, standing only two feet away from it, with Monsignor Vacchini carefully angling his light to bring out the shallow
scratches, she was surprised and puzzled by what she saw, even
a little shocked.

There were indeed many names, crowding against and over
one another, along with prayers and invocations. These her practiced eye was readily able to pick out from the tangle. But she
was abruptly struck by another element, something very odd,
but which had received no comment in the report. In most of
the names, almost every individual letter was heavily festooned
with additional short scratches, seemingly random lines trailing
off at all angles and crisscrossing each other haphazardly. Even
the spaces between the names and words, above and below,
which would ordinarily have been blank, were filled with this
strangely web-like pattern of strung-together lines. The total
effect was one of rampant confusion, almost mindless, yet with
an underlying, if not quite definable, feeling of purpose.

This was a sight which, in all her pursuit of ancient inscriptions, Dr. Guarducci had never before encountered. In the catacombs and other early Christian cemeteries, the walls at many
points had been covered by epigraphs. But in none of these were
the inscriptions so heaped up, or embedded in such an angry
matrix of inextricable lines.

After a long, puzzled look, she abruptly turned aside, as if
afraid of becoming too fascinated. Her professional schedule
was already far overcrowded with work. There were articles
waiting to be written, lectures to deliver, field trips to make. She
had set aside these few days for the Valerius inscription only because, if it could be deciphered, it seemed to promise some information of value. But there would be no opportunity for further involvement.

Alone in the Valerius tomb, armed with a light, a large magnifying glass, and a notebook, Dr. Guarducci began a close inspection of the faded Latin words. The first phrase, she found, was
still readily legible, though she now saw something else that had
not been made clear in the report, and which would add to the

difficulties. The sizes of the letters, and their general shapes, differed markedly, and the spacing between them was quite at random. The first line of the inscription was even interrupted, broken in two, by the sketched head of Peter.

To the left of the chin were the letters PETRU, while to the right were several other letters: SROGA ☥ XSIHS. Beyond any doubt, this was meant to be a single line and could be read as PETRUS ROGA CHRISTUS JESU, which translated to "Peter pray Christ Jesus . . ." The small, roundheaded cross was easily identifiable as the *ankh*, the Egyptian symbol of salvation, which in this period was often used by Christians.

Just underneath, in another line, were the letters PRO-SANC   S. This required a restoration of two letters in the gap between the C and the S, and became PRO SANCTIS, "for the holy . . ."

Three more lines followed, one below the other, and it was these lines which had not yet been satisfactorily unraveled. Since their first discovery, several tentative readings had been suggested, but none had been found convincing, and interest in the problem had steadily waned. That the three lines should breed uncertainty was no wonder, thought Dr. Guarducci. Erratic letter sizes, wavering lines, gaps which might indicate either faded letters or blank spaces, made them extremely difficult even to trace out, leaving wide room for doubt.

With infinite patience, for hours at a time, she painstakingly followed through her magnifying glass the broken or twisted or misshapen strokes of each individual letter. Frequently, she was misled by the badly mottled plaster and the spreading network of fine, dirt-filled cracks, not always at first realizing her mistake. Noting down each letter as it yielded up its shape, or what appeared to be its shape, she came to the end of the last line three days after starting, confident that no minutest trace of red lead or charcoal clung to the surface beyond. Then she turned to study her notes:

HOM   BUS
CRESTIANUS D
CO PUSTUUMSEP

Only a few minutes were required to reconstruct and translate these phrases, and her heart jumped as the meaning became clear: HOMINIBUS CRESTIANUS AD CORPUS TUUM SEPULTIS—"Christian men buried near your body." The necropolis had finally yielded a definite reference to Peter's remains as lying in the vicinity. The grave under the high altar was little more than thirty feet from the Valerius tomb.

In the following days, as Dr. Guarducci talked eagerly of her discovery with other experts, it became evident that its true value was more a matter of corroboration, rather than of original proof. The crux lay in the dating. In her view, from various indications the writing of the inscription could be assigned to a period straddling the third and fourth centuries, say, 290–310. It thus attested the presence of Peter's remains even before the advent of Constantine, and nicely filled in the century following the mention of the Tropaion by the priest Gaius.

Other scholars, while complimenting her on a brilliant feat of decipherment, disagreed with her dating. The scrawl was a veritable defacement of the shrine, they pointed out, as well as an open avowal of Christian sentiment. As such, it could hardly have been done while the tomb was still operative and in pagan hands. Only after condemnation of the entire necropolis, in preparation for the first basilica, perhaps sometime about 330, would any Christian have dared to mark a pagan tomb in this fashion. In that case, the inscription became part of the general evidence linked directly to Constantine's operations. Immensely intriguing, even reassuring, it still was not of independent worth.

In reality, the true value of Dr. Guarducci's work with the Valerius inscription lay in quite another direction. Almost predictably, its hard challenge had kindled her latent curiosity about the whole matter of the excavations, and with Peter's grave in particular. Not long afterward, despite a determined effort to put the basilica with all its scientific enticements out of her mind, her thoughts began reaching back to the graffiti wall. Soon she was burning to know what purpose, if any, could possibly be served by that giddy mass of extraneous, apparently senseless lines. Her request for permission to make a study of the intriguing tangle was quickly honored, but she was delayed for a while by some other commitments, and by the writing of a report on the Valerius epigraph. It was September 1953 before she was able to begin.

As her first move at the graffiti wall, Dr. Guarducci arranged for a series of professional photographs to be taken of the whole surface, overlapping close-ups which would capture every nuance of the inscriptions. Spending hours each day at the wall, usually kneeling on a cushion, one hand holding a light while the other wielded the magnifying glass, she was soon oblivious to the passing hours. As the days went by she fell into a steady rhythm, spending mornings at the basilica, then continuing her studies with the photographs at home in the afternoons, the only break in the routine coming from her teaching duties at the university. There were also frequent visits to the libraries and museums of Rome as she searched for any smallest light that might be thrown on the scratches by the work of the other scholars in related fields.

To her great consternation, the first weeks of this intensive effort, in which she tried one hypothesis after another while calling on her whole store of epigraphical knowledge, yielded exactly nothing. Behind the enigmatic jumble she could discern no rationale, no pattern. No ghost of a personality became visible. Only here and there could she find some letter—an A, a B, an E—which appeared to separate itself from its surroundings. Or were these forms mere accidents of conjunction? Of even this she couldn't be certain, and when a whole month fled by without the least hint of progress, in desperation she began casting around for something, anything, some stray bit of information, that might afford even the slightest clue to the wall's stubborn secret.

It was now, in the face of Dr. Guarducci's threatened defeat, that the perverse fate which had so seriously flawed the original investigation more than a decade before, at last began to make amends. As the frustrated scholar arrived at the site one morning, occupied at a task nearby was the workman Giovanni

Segoni. Now promoted to head foreman of the Sampietrini, he
and Dr. Guarducci had already met once or twice, but only in
passing. This particular morning's encounter would be different.

After greeting each other, for no special reason the two stood
looking at the graffiti wall, remarking casually on the inscriptions. As they talked, Dr. Guarducci's eyes trailed down to the
enlarged opening of the repository, its brittle edges now plas-
tered to prevent further deterioration. Had anything been found
in this space, she wondered, which might help with the inscriptions? The official report in its very short and cursory account
had specified that the cavity had been found empty except for a
few bits of bone, some minor debris, and the coin of Limoges.
But had that been all? Had anything else turned up, perhaps
some object apparently of no worth, which had been left un-
listed by the archaeologists? In her groping for aid she was unwilling to dismiss even this unlikely possibility. Segoni, she
recalled, had taken part in the excavations from the very start.

"Tell me, Giovanni," she said, pointing, "do you remember
what sorts of things were found inside that cavity?"

Segoni looked down at the opening and thought for a moment. "Yes, I emptied it myself," he answered, "when old Monsignor Kaas gave the order. I can show you the things if you
want."

Not waiting for a reply, Segoni turned and led the way along
a series of corridors until he came to a door which swung open
on a small, dimly lit storeroom tucked into an angle behind the
chapel of St. Columban. Spread round on tables, shelves, and
much of the floor were dozens of boxes, wooden or metal, of
many shapes and sizes. Most of these boxes, Segoni explained as
he moved round the room opening one after another, held bones
and other things turned up in the early digging. He still didn't
know what was to be done with them all.

"Here," he said at last, lifting a box to a table, "this is it." He
handed Dr. Guarducci a small card which was slightly torn and
rather limp from dampness. Smoothing it carefully on the table,
she was able to make out three words written in faded pencil:
"*ossa—urna—graf.*"

The box, made of wood, was carried by Segoni to an empty office nearby where there was less clutter and more light. Placing it on a table beside a window, he removed several clamps. Dr. Guarducci lifted the cover off, looked in, then stared for a moment in some doubt. Instead of a meager collection of bone fragments, the "slight remains" vaguely described by the excavators, the box held a considerable pile of bones, quite a few of which could hardly be described as slight.

Gingerly, Dr. Guarducci took up the larger pieces and laid them one by one on the table. Five were of some length, measuring from six to ten inches, all showing partial decay. It was obvious that they had come from human arms or legs. There were also a half dozen pieces from a human spinal column, vertebrae easily recognizable, and several thicker, knobbed pieces which might have belonged to knee or elbow joints. Almost a hundred other, smaller pieces of broken or decayed bone, of various shapes and thicknesses, were in the box, some several inches long but many of a size that could only be called tiny. On a closer look she saw that, in color, the larger pieces and a few of the smaller ones were a stark white, while other pieces ranged from duller white to yellowish to varying shades of brown.

Aside from the bones, the box yielded nothing that gave promise of helping with the decipherment. There were three or four bits of red plaster and of marble, and some dozen diminutive shreds of decaying fabric, colored a washed-out reddish-brown, in which still glinted purplish highlights and gold threads. There were also two corroded coins, one of which was identifiable as belonging to the Middle Ages, a fact which lent support to the earlier contention of the four excavators that the repository had been opened in the tenth or eleventh century. The second coin was judged to be too much worn for proper identification.

Fleetingly, Dr. Guarducci wondered again how the excavators could have described the bones in the box as "slight." Kirschbaum in his own writings had even used the word "splinters," a term which was wholly inadequate. Questioning Segoni, she

asked if he were certain that everything in the box had come
from the graffiti wall. Emphatically, the workman replied that
he had emptied the space with his own hands while Monsignor
Kaas stood by. He had then written out that very label at the
Monsignor's direction. The box had been carefully locked and
deposited in the storeroom, which had also been kept locked, the
Monsignor being very particular about such things. The box,
Segoni was positive, had never been touched since. Everything
in it at that moment had definitely come from the cavity in the
graffiti wall ten years before.

The question that had begun to rise in Dr. Guarducci's mind,
never quite formed, now began to fade. If these bones had held
no interest for the four original investigators, she reasoned, then
they were evidently of slight importance. If the marble repository had indeed been opened in medieval times—and there
seemed little doubt of it—the bones must date to that period, or
at least they had been laid into the repository at that time. If
older, they would naturally be of more interest, though in what
way it was hard to tell.

In any case, it now seemed quite clear, definite in fact, that
the bones in the box must comprise the remains of several individuals. Undoubtedly they were stray bones from different
graves turned up accidentally in the vicinity from time to time
and together enclosed in the graffiti wall as a convenient os-
suarium. Some sort of connection with the ninth-century Saracen
invaders appeared likely. More to the point, there was nothing
here that could help with the inscriptions—a disappointing outcome.

Returning the bones to the box, she wrapped the box itself in
heavy brown paper, then tied it round with stout cord. Simply
as a matter of scientific precision, she had decided that these
unrecorded items should sooner or later be examined by experts,
and meantime they ought to be kept secure. With Monsignor
Vacchini's permission, the box was not put back in the damp
storeroom, but was carried to the basilica's main offices, where it
was locked in a cupboard.

8

What the Graffiti Hid

From the strange embroidery on the graffiti wall, under Dr. Guarducci's questing stare some fifty names eventually emerged, distinct and separate, all of them familiar in third- and fourth-century Roman usage. About half were linked to a Christ monogram, and about a third included prayers and invocations, always abbreviated, wishing for the dead eternal joy in Christ. But even after isolating all these names and phrases, often by minutely tracing out individual letters in succession, there still remained the weird inundation of extra lines from which no sense could be extracted.

Further weeks of fruitless study passed, then months, and despite the many fatiguing hours she spent on her knees before the wall, or bent over the pile of photographs at home, her bafflement continued to deepen. Earnest discussion of the vexing problem with her sister, with colleagues at the university, and with Pope Pius himself, brought sympathy and encouragement but no real assistance. Once during those months, however, her efforts were rewarded with a discovery, and though it proved of no assistance in deciphering the other scratches, in its own way it was electrifying.

When for the twentieth time her magnifying glass moved across the upper left corner of the graffiti wall, there suddenly leaped out at her, just above a Christ monogram, five letters arranged in two lines:

HO
VIN

At their right edges both lines ran into broken plaster and could thus have once been longer. In fact, the ragged form of what might have been a C still clung vaguely to the end of the first line. Instantly Dr. Guarducci recognized the phrase for what it was, the only thing it could be: IN HOC VINCE, Latin for "In this, conquer." These very words, she knew, had formed part of Constantine's famous aerial vision in the year 312, just before his final battle for Rome. In the vision, the words had been accompanied by some unspecified type of cross, and the Emperor had jubilantly ordered his troops to paint the emblem on their shields and helmets. A rapid victory had followed.

As it happened, the earliest report of this memorable incident was a contemporary one, written down from Constantine's own lips by the historian Eusebius. In his short account, and almost as an afterthought, Eusebius had also preserved the vital fact that the Emperor had not been the only witness to the arresting sight: "He said that with his own eyes, during the afternoon, while the day was already fading, he had seen a shining cross in the sky, more brilliant than the sun, accompanied by the words, 'In this, conquer.' He remained stunned by the vision, and so did all the army following him in the expedition, which had also seen the miracle."

The marvel had quickly become an accepted part of church history and had remained so, unquestioned, for many centuries. More recently, there had arisen a tendency among scholars to question its factual basis. Some preferred to explain it as spurious, a later addition to Eusebius' writings. Others had gone so far as to suggest that Eusebius himself might have simply invented the whole incident. But here on the graffiti wall was an occurrence of the famous phrase which certainly antedated the historian's work. Its presence could only mean that knowledge of the vision, in all its compelling reality, had been current among

Roman Christians long before Eusebius wrote. A decade, at most, separated inscription and vision, but the interval might easily have been a good deal less, even as little as a year or two. It might indeed—and the possibility was enough to send a shiver through the scholar—have actually been cut into the wall by an eyewitness to the memorable event.

By now Dr. Guarducci had become convinced that the enigmatic scratches *must* hide some rational meaning, and the conviction, based more on instinct than observation, was enough to keep her doggedly at work. Able to pick out several more letters from the tangle, she had been intrigued to note that some of them—A, V, or N—appeared actually to be repeated within themselves. In other instances, it seemed, certain letters had been altered in form by the deft addition of one or more lines.

The first real clue, when it finally showed up, revealed itself in a totally unexpected way, in an aspect of early Christianity already familiar, but which on the wall had been transposed into something quite unfamiliar. Small as the clue was, it provided the indispensable mechanism needed to bridge the gap between known and unknown.

Fairly frequently on the wall there occurred the well-documented *alpha-omega* combination, AO (in Greek AΩ). This was a favorite device of early Christians in which the first and last letters of the Greek alphabet were used to indicate God or the Savior. The sign had been derived in the first instance from St. John's Apocalypse, where the symbolism is pronounced by the voice of God: "I am the Alpha and the Omega, the first and the last, the beginning and the end." In use since at least the start of the second century, the device had spread with the church across the Mediterranean and into the East. Its appearance among the graffiti thus was hardly noteworthy in itself, but Dr. Guarducci now noticed that it was used with a difference.

Examining the name MARIA, she saw that to the left of the letter I there was scratched a tiny omega sign, ω. Leading from this small insertion, another scratched line curved over the top of the I and connected with the final A of the name. Here, it appeared, was an AO in reverse, a curious inversion, if deliberate.

When she saw that the same reversal occurred on several other parts of the wall—written even more plainly as an inserted ΩA—she concluded that the anomaly was no accident. "Beginning-and-End" transformed to "End-and-Beginning"?

In a Christian context, the only plausible interpretation for such a phrase was a reference to bodily death as the start of eternal life. That was reasonable enough in the framework of early Christian thought, but it made the OA a twofold symbol, one in which the original meaning had been extended. Ultimately, perhaps, it became a reference to Christ as the one through whose own death and resurrection, salvation had been made possible for all. Death in Christ was the beginning of true life.

Hesitating, Dr. Guarducci found herself wondering why she had never before encountered this symbolic reversal of the alpha-omega. Had others known of it? A few days of study in the libraries of Rome brought a quick answer: the reversal had indeed been noted before by a few isolated scholars, in funerary inscriptions. But it had received little serious attention. Most had dismissed it as a hurried or indifferent form of the ubiquitous AΩ, perhaps even an error. None had been sufficiently impressed by the peculiarity to make it a subject of separate study.

Unwilling to dismiss this rare symbol as meaningless, Dr. Guarducci reasoned that if it was indeed purposeful, a kind of cryptographic variation of the original, then perhaps other marks on the wall might be couched in a similar code. Once again she began systematically gleaning through the massed scratches, both at the wall and in the more manageable photographs. This time supporting evidence started to show up almost immediately.

The T, a known symbol for the cross in antiquity, was several times spotlighted in such a way as to leave little doubt of its symbolic function. The same thing was evident with the X, an early designation for Christ. More than once the phrase IN ☧ (in Christ), was varied to IN A, making the A interchangeable with the monogram. The tripling of the A, which she had noted earlier, now suddenly took on a quite specific meaning—did it not suggest a reference to the Holy Trinity? And could it be only by chance that where the monogram for Christ, second person of the Trinity, was added to these triplings, it was clearly attached to the *second* A?

Haunting libraries, delving into the works of archaeologists and church historians, sorting through long-neglected artifacts and old documents in museums, Dr. Guarducci gradually accumulated a list of meanings, definite or highly probable, for a whole range of letters. Among them were E for *Eden*, F for *Son* (Latin *fidelius*), N for *Victory* (Greek *nika*), R for *Resurrection*, S for *Health* (Latin *salut*), V for *Life* (Latin *vita*). The capital letter A was abundantly confirmed—through its use in mosaics and paintings which had never been quite understood before— as standing for Christ. The letter M, or letters MA, indicating Mary the mother of Christ, offered a particularly impressive example. Nestled inside the M there was often an A (Greek form Λ), which served as the last letter of MARIA, and also stood for her Son, ӍӍ .

No one, she found, had ever made any sustained investigation of this alphabetical symbolism, though it seemed to have been rather widely employed among Christians in the second and third centuries. In no sense a formal or standardized practice, this spiritual cryptography had grown and spread haphazardly over the decades, no doubt in response to the pressing need to keep certain revealing beliefs hidden from hostile pagan neighbors and officials. But also at work, Dr. Guarducci felt, was a definite inclination in the ancient world, among both Christians and pagans, toward a kind of artifice, a taste for the arcane, in which the appeal of religious beliefs was enhanced by a veiling of mysticism. There was also the prevailing Roman habit, often carried to an unreadable extreme, of sharply abbreviating names and familiar words in public inscriptions.

Like a bright flare bursting over a nighttime landscape, the nascent theory of mystical cryptography now brilliantly lit up the darkness of the graffiti wall. As finally formulated by Dr. Guarducci, the code was threefold. First, there was simple letter symbolism, in which almost every letter of the alphabet carried a special meaning. Usually employing the initial letter of a word, the message could be endlessly varied by direct or indirect combinations, according to the ingenuity of the writer. Second, there was letter transfiguration, in which by the careful addition of lines to an existing letter, several concepts could be expressed simultaneously in a confined space. Here too the possibilities were limited only by the writer's cleverness. Third, there was linkage, in which different letters located handily near each other could be joined by the drawing of straight or curved lines to form still other combinations.

Using this simple code, the faithful visiting the site had been able to express themselves with an astonishing range of ideas. Out of the scratches overlying the fifty names, Dr. Guarducci was eventually able to disentangle, among others, references to Christ as God and Son of God, the victory of the cross, Christ as the Resurrection and the Life, Christ and his mother in paradise, life eternal, the Holy Trinity, peace and salvation in Christ, and Christ as the Light of the World. This fantastic network of meandering lines was in reality a marvelously living document, preserving in a unique immediacy the spiritual hunger of that generation of Christians which was first to emerge from the long night of suppression and persecution.

But what of Peter? In this abundant flowering of spiritual sentiment on the wall guarding his grave, had the chief apostle been ignored?

Almost from the moment in which she first glimpsed the wall's secret, Dr. Guarducci had confidently expected that, in some manner, Peter would be mentioned. Eagerly on the alert as she threaded her way through the coded abbreviations, she had not searched long before she encounterd the letters PE worked into a Christ monogram rising above the O in the name VENE-ROSA, ☧ . The way in which the Greek letter *rho* or R (P) was here made to serve as the Latin letter P, had thrown her off the trail at first, but she soon discovered that the substitution was not new. It had been seen several times before, in the catacombs and on old medallions, though never in connection with

Peter. When she found the same device on the wall a second time, embroidered on the L of LEONIA, this time with the E attached to the downstroke, ✗ she knew that the mysterious absence of Peter's name on his own grave had been solved.

In abbreviated form, the apostle's name was present on the wall at least twenty times, usually accompanied by prayers for the dead person named—in one case expressing joy that the lost relative lay in the same cemetery that held Peter's own body. On every part of the wall—freestanding between the letters of a name, formed from or engrafted onto existing lines—there occurred the initials PE or PET. Often they were preceded by an A, in this case short for the Latin *ad*, meaning *near* (perhaps also denoting a link with Christ). Most often the initials were arranged as a monogram, a device for designating Peter which was entirely new to historians: ℞ or ℞ . Revealingly, the abbreviation was often associated with the Christ monogram, so interwoven as to suggest an unusually close union between Redeemer and apostle. Significantly, in two cases this union of symbols had added to it the name of Maria.

It was while researching the Peter monogram in libraries and museums that Dr. Guarducci uncovered still another fact largely forgotten over the centuries. It brought dramatically to light a fuller picture of Peter's true position in early Christianity.

The unusual monogram, its link to Peter totally unrecognized, had actually been found before, outside the Vatican, and it had by no means been confined to funerary inscriptions. Surprisingly, it could be found scratched on ancient monuments, inked onto old documents of all kinds, worked subtly into wall mosaics, incised on the margins of public signs, roughly stamped on medals, coins, rings, statuettes, pots and similar household wares, even painted on gaming boards. The occurrence of the device in so many areas of Roman life unrelated to religion was, in fact, a minor phenomenon which had bedeviled classical scholars for years. The occasional attempts to explain it had not succeeded, and most experts were inclined to shrug it off as some obscure type of pagan good-luck symbol, its origin irretrievably lost in the dim past.

Now, with its discovery on the graffiti wall, there could be no real doubt of the symbol's true meaning—and no doubt whatever as to its origin. "I will give you the keys of the kingdom of heaven," Jesus had declared to Peter, and the Roman faithful had obviously delighted in the way the key-like monogram so precisely reflected those words.

But this pervasive use of the Peter symbol in secular Roman circles told a still more engrossing tale. Even centuries after the apostle's death, and though his place had been taken by a series of other impressive figures, this first pope had continued to haunt the thoughts of later Christians, growing ever dearer in their memories as the long, slow decades of persecution rolled by. Peter, above all, remained their earthly link to Christ. In their harried and yearning hearts, he had continued to be the one man who could bring them close to the healing personality of Jesus. Through Peter, they could stand in spirit on the blessed shores of Galilee as the eternal words of the Master fell through the crisp air, as they had when first spoken, like a benediction. Now it could be seen that the historian Eusebius had told only the literal truth about Peter, then dead some two and a half centuries, when he wrote: "He was known throughout the world, even in the western countries, and his memory among the Romans is still more alive today than the memory of all those who lived before him."

Dr. Guarducci had brought her task to a triumphant conclusion, but it had been the most demanding labor of her career. When starting work on the graffiti wall she had estimated that it might occupy her for several weeks, perhaps a month. Instead, counting preparation of a heavily illustrated, three-volume report, it had absorbed nearly all her mental and physical energies, and filled a large part of her waking hours, for five long years.

9

The Bones Examined

Three lead-lined wooden boxes lay open on a long table in a bare, isolated room at the basilica. In them were carefully stored the bones that had been found in the central grave, those dug by Father Kirschbaum from under the triangular rise in the red wall. Standing before the table, a white laboratory smock covering his street clothes, was a sober-faced, middle-aged man named Venerando Correnti. One of Europe's most distinguished anthropologists, a leading member of the faculty at Palermo University, Professor Correnti was preparing to make a full-scale anatomical study of the bones now widely believed to be those of the aspotle.

Ever since their discovery fourteen years before, the red wall bones had been preserved in the Pope's own apartment. Dutifully safeguarded, they still had not been accorded any special marks of reverence. Instead, for scholars and churchmen alike, they had continued to be a source of severe frustration.

The bones had been taken from what was incontestably Peter's own original grave (the portion disturbed by the building of the red wall). They had been medically certified as belonging to a single individual, someone who, like Peter, had been an elderly man of powerful build. In the opinion of many, this was proof enough, prompting a strong desire to have the remains declared authentic. Of course, more rounded evidence would have been welcome, these advocates admitted, but its absence should not be allowed to obscure undoubted facts.

On the other hand, as cooler minds recognized, there were still too many imponderables to allow any such authoritative step. The bones had been found strangely heaped together in the bare earth below the wall. Obviously, they had already been disturbed at least once, a fact that raised doubts about what other interference the grave and its contents might have suffered in the centuries before the erection of the first basilica. No less troubling was the ninth-century sack of the basilica, and perhaps the tomb, by the Saracens. Such a doubtful provenance, in itself, gave quite ample reason for pause.

In reality, it was pointed out more than once, lacking as they did all intrinsic evidence, the only way the bones could definitely be tied to Peter would have been the presence in them of some disease or deformity known to have been suffered by the apostle. But nowhere in the existing documents regarding Peter was any physical infirmity recorded.

For conscientious men, this situation had posed an extremely uncomfortable dilemma, and in the end it had reduced the authorities to frustrated inaction. Since the first, brief noncommittal mention of the bones in the official report, no further information had appeared in print, a silence which for scholars and churchmen around the world had grown steadily more exasperating.

Because of the Vatican's indecision, it was charged, the belief was rapidly becoming fixed that the bones really *were* those of Peter—worse, even the four excavators had begun to lend themselves openly to this lamentable process of approval by default. Kirschbaum's published opinion, for example, often came unwarrantably, and unwisely, close to certitude. "A recess under the lowest niche of the red wall," he had written, "was found to contain the bones of a man of advanced years and powerful build. The skull was missing. Who, we may well ask, is this old man in St. Peter's grave? In view of the fact that the head of the apostle has for many centuries been preserved and venerated in the

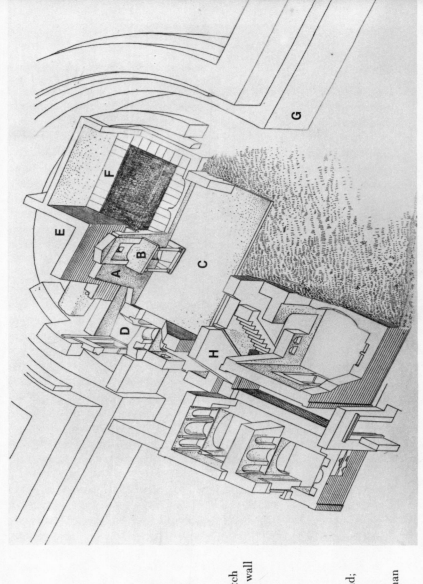

17. Overhead view (sketch reconstruction) of the red wall complex.

A) the red wall;
B) the Tropaion;
C) the tiled courtyard;
D) the alleyway;
E) the anteroom;
F) the upper burial ground;
G) the foundation of Constantine's basilica;
H) start of the line of Roman tombs.

18.   The original second-century entrance to the alleyway behind the red
wall, with doorposts and sill of travertine still in place. The door itself was
probably removed in the fourth century by Constantine's workmen.

19. The alleyway behind the red wall (seen farther in on the right) after excavation. The brick walls along the left are the remains of the Agricola tomb (foreground) and the curious anteroom to its rear. The marble sarcophagus is a burial which was let down through the floor of the basilica many centuries later.

20. The alley side of the red wall, which cuts across Peter's grave. The concrete bench (lower left) stands over the filled-in portion of the grave. The brick wall to the right of the vertical seam belongs to a Roman tomb erected about A.D. 130.

21. A few of the second- and third-century graves discovered by the excavators surrounding the central chamber, reflecting an early desire for burial near Peter. Eventually, about thirty such graves were found in the area, some containing bones but most holding only dust.

22.   A model reconstruction of the Tropaion, built into the red wall over Peter's grave about A.D. 150–60, less than a century after his death. Spread before the Tropaion was a tiled courtyard.

23. The graffiti wall standing beside and above Peter's grave, as it appeared soon after it was uncovered. The opening into the secret marble repository is seen at the bottom. When first found, this opening was only a narrow slit.

24. Close-up of a portion of the graffiti wall (its upper right corner), showing the tangled mass of inscriptions. The names *Victor* and *Gaudentia* can be read at the center. The word *speci*, faintly visible at the lower right, refers to Peter's grave.

Lateran church, the conclusion that these are the bones of the apostle himself is well nigh irresistible."

Perhaps, critics contended, it was only natural that the excavators and others close to the work should, in these peculiar circumstances, allow the weight of their beliefs to fall on the positive side. And of course it was only to be expected that many of the faithful should willingly follow their lead. But this was scarcely the path of science.

By the spring of 1956, this widespread concern over the unresolved question, coupled with the Vatican's own growing desire to have it settled, had brought about a determination to take some definite action. The long period of indecision finally came to an end when Pope Pius XII directed the basilica's new administrator, Monsignor Primo Principi, to pursue the only course left open. The bones were to be reexamined, this time not by medical doctors but by the best qualified specialist available. Whatever the results, they were to be promptly published.

If nothing but corroboration of the earlier conclusions were achieved, the problem would still not be wholly settled. But there then might be more reason, and a greater willingness among scholars, to accept the remains as those of Peter. If authenticity were in some definite manner to be disproved, at least the truth would have been served.

Lifting the bones one after another from the boxes and placing them on the table, Professor Correnti peered closely at each in turn. Even before the boxes were emptied, he knew that his task would be an unusually long and difficult one. Too many important bones were missing, or were present only in fragments.

If an entire, well-preserved skeleton had been available, it would have been relatively simple to determine such things as age at death, sex, height, and body type. The investigation would still have consumed a good deal of time, with many fine measurements and other tests required for each of several dozen bones. But the process would have gone smoothly and steadily, and the results, most often, would have been entirely dependable. When certain crucial bones were missing, however, or were altered and reduced by decay, then the work became endlessly laborious, requiring infinitely more time. The results, too, would be less satisfactory.

According to the number and type of bones present, and their condition, the conclusions reached would have to be expressed with lessening degrees of precision, in such terms as *almost certain, probable, presumable,* all the way down to *indeterminable.* From what Correnti had been able to judge in his first review, it appeared to him that little more than half the skeleton was present, with very few of the bones intact.

To one side of the table, the scientist gathered the larger bones and fragments, carefully spreading them. The smaller pieces he arranged to the other side. Among the larger ones, he began to check off those he could recognize on sight. There was a nearly whole sternum (breastbone), five pieces of the ilium (pelvic girdle), a complete left tibia (shinbone), and the left patella (kneecap). Suddenly he stopped counting and stared. On the table lay *three* fibulas. These were the long, slight bones of the lower leg, which paralleled the heavier tibia from knee to ankle. But each leg of a human being contained only one of these.

Looking through the gathering of smaller bones, Correnti patiently separated out a number which were recognizable as the metatarsals (from the foot, just above the toes). Carefully counting, he soon saw that there were far too many of these small bones for one person. Picking up a chunky fragment identifiable as part of the left humerus (shoulder), he looked along the table and after some minutes spotted a similar piece from the same area of the skeleton—and a few seconds later came across still another.

The most conspicuous bone on the table was the left tibia, about twelve inches long, intact and well preserved. Correnti next assembled a second tibia, which had been broken in two at its middle. Then, after searching for a while among the larger fragments, he found parts of what he judged to be four additional tibias. There could be no doubt of it. On the table lay the bones of not one but several individuals.

Almost immediately another surprise showed up. Many of the bones, those pieces darker in hue, had come from animals. There were bones from cows, horses, goats, and sheep, perhaps as many as fifty or sixty pieces in all, making about a fourth of the total spread on the table. After a bemused look at these bones, Correnti set them aside in order to concentrate on the human remains.

The examination now entered a phase which was to prove of weary length. To separate the various individuls, and to determine the basic facts of sex, age at death, and body type for each, a long series of fine measurements was required on all of the nearly two hundred remaining bones. Each of these measurements had to be recorded, and then checked against standard anatomical tables. The measurements themselves, and the other tests for such vital factors as porosity and degree of softening (sponginess), were by no means simple. In settling the age of a single bone, for example, the medullary canal (the tube-like cavity at the center of the longer bones) had to be gauged for width in order to find the amount of deterioration, a chore easily enough accomplished when the bone or fragment was well preserved. Where there was only a trace of the canal in a broken or decayed piece, the measurements became increasingly more exacting.

According to the amount of time given to it, the task could stretch out for many months, even years, and with Professor Correnti the situation was aggravated. Because of his teaching commitments at the University of Palermo, and regular appointments as guest lecturer at other leading schools, his availability was limited. Further, all the work had to be done at the basilica, since the bones were not to be allowed out of the Vatican. Under these circumstances, as it developed, Correnti's assignment was to be drawn out to unusual lengths, and several years passed before he had completed even the determination of age at death. After that, however, sorting of the bones went rapidly.

There were just three persons present, he concluded. At death, two of them had probably been in their fifties. The third individual, to whom most of the bones belonged, could have been seventy years old or more.

For determination of the sexes, a delicate procedure, most of the necessary bones appeared to be present, but all had been fractured in one way or another, and most were only small fragments. Fortunately, for one of the most important bones, the pelvic girdle, there were a half dozen fairly substantial pieces. Patiently measuring each piece in several different ways, constantly comparing values with standard anthropological charts listing the ranges of male and female characteristics, Correnti found himself well into 1960 before the task was completed.

The two individuls in their fifties, he decided, were probably both males. One was of medium build, the other robust. For the slighter man, several fragments of the skull were present, and to him also belonged five teeth found in the box. Because of the much larger number of bones available for the elderly individual, the sex could be judged with greater precision, though the results still fell short of absolute. The third person was, almost certainly, a female.

These results were communicated to the Vatican verbally, in advance of the official report. Understandably, they caused heavy gloom. The presence of the animal bones troubled no one, however, for it was pointed out that the basilica itself stood very near, perhaps even partially atop, the site of the first-century *circus* or arena of Nero, the traditional location of Peter's crucifixion. Here, in the first century, many animals had been stabled, and in addition the area was known to have accommodated a number of farms. In these circumstances, the fact that certain animal bones had somehow become mixed with the human remains seemed almost a guarantee of the original grave. The animal skeletons had probably been lying beneath the soil when the grave was first dug. Perhaps they had been picked up with the human bones, in ignorance, as the grave was being shortened at the building of the red wall. A much more devastating blow than the presence of animal bones was the determination that the elderly individual was female.

Still, there were some in the Vatican who refused to concede. The provisional nature of the negative judgment, they insisted, left the question at least partially open. The elderly person—for whom a skull was entirely absent—had been classed as "almost certainly" female. This description, patently, was not conclusive, especially on so vexed and sensitive a question. The issue had simply shifted from "probably Peter," to its opposite, "probably not Peter."

The few random bones of the other two men could easily be explained. Most likely they had entered the apostle's grave by accident, perhaps moved by soil slippage over the centuries, perhaps in the same way as the animal bones. All had been gathered up together by pious hands, when the cache was made beneath the red wall, in fear of losing any portion of Peter's body. So long as there was even a slight chance that these were the bones of the apostle, the dilemma remained.

Professor Correnti, his work done, kept aloof from the discussion. He was, in any case, busy preparing his report for publication. It would contain, in addition to the general findings, all the background materials, lengthy tables in which every bone and fragment would be listed and described, charts setting forth all measurements made on each bone no matter how small, comparisons with the standard tables, and a full set of detailed photographs. Merely to complete the excavation record, he had also agreed to perform a similar study on some other bones found in the vicinity. He would examine the few which had been dug up from the courtyard in front of the Tropaion, and also those which had been removed by Monsignor Kaas from the graffiti wall.

After a leisurely six months, Correnti reported that the courtyard bones belonged to four individuals. Three were adults, of indeterminable age and sex, the fourth was probably a male, probably about forty years old. In this group also, many animal bones were present, of the same species found among the red wall bones, a fact that bolstered the assertion that the whole area had been used to inter the carcasses of dead animals.

It was October 1962 before Correnti, glad to see the end of an interminable assignment, turned his attention to the wooden box with the brown paper wrapping.

Led to believe that the graffiti wall cache held a varied mix of individuals, Correnti was mildly surprised when he could find no duplication among the bones spread before him on the table, duplication such as had been quickly evident with the red wall bones. If there was a mixture here it would show up only after each item had been analyzed for age and sex.

Almost none of the bones on the table was whole. Except for three very small pieces, all had been eaten away by decay. The total number was 135, but only a half dozen of these were of some length, six inches or more, with the best-preserved being the longer bones from the legs. Conspicuous on the table were the left and right femur (thighbone), the left and right tibia (shinbone), and the right fibula (lower leg).

There were also some animal bones, but much fewer comparatively than had occurred with the first two groups, only some dozen pieces in all, none large. Another dozen very slight and fragile pieces proved to be the complete skeleton of a field mouse. Probably the little creature had entered alive into the repository, Correnti reasoned, and then, unable to find its way out, had died there. The condition of these mouse bones—very desiccated and stark white—seemed to show that they had never lain in the earth. Further, it was unlikely that all the tiny pieces would still be present if they had been transferred by hand.

As the scientist's enumeration of the human remains continued he began to see that, except for the feet, every part of the skeleton was represented. For the skull there were some twenty-seven fragments of the cranium, along with two small pieces of the mandible (jaw), and one tooth, a lower-left canine. One of the cranial pieces bore a trace of the suture, and since this was completely ossified Correnti could tell immediately that the skull, in any case, was that of an individual at least fifty years old, and probably a great deal older.

There were eight arm fragments, upper and lower, making

about a quarter of the total lengths of left and right arms. Interestingly, the hands were well represented, even though most of the finger bones were very small and might easily have been lost or overlooked. The left hand was virtually complete; the right lacked two fingers and most of the wrist. For the legs, both thighs and shins, about eighty percent of the bone was present, though in fragments. Only the feet, from the ankles down, were entirely missing. Not a single one of the many small bones to be found in the human foot could be seen on the table.

Several months were needed to determine the age at death for all the bones, a task that was not finished until early in 1963. Without exception, they fell within the category of "elderly," between sixty and seventy years. An even longer period was required to determine the sex, as Correnti made nearly a hundred separate measurements and other analyses on more than two dozen critical fragments. In the end he had no doubt of his opinion, though because the skeleton was incomplete his description had to be a qualified one. The bones from the graffiti wall, he concluded, were those of a single, elderly individual, about five feet seven inches tall, of heavy build, and almost certainly male.

A thorough investigator, in his report Correnti also mentioned two further facts which had struck him. In the depressions and hollows of many of the pieces he had found encrusted soil, earth particles clinging in hardened patches. From this, he said, it was reasonable to suppose that the bones had lain—and for a considerable period of time—in a bare earth grave.

The second fact was still more curious. Four or five of the larger bones showed an unnatural staining on their intact extremities. The color was a dark, uncertain red, in spots tending to reddish-brown, the same as could be seen in the shreds of fabric found in the wooden box. All these bones, it appeared, at some time after dissolution of the flesh, had been taken from the earth and wrapped in a purplish, gold-threaded cloth.

10

The Peter Theory

Pope Pius XII, after reigning for almost twenty years, died in October 1958. To his own grave he carried one of the sharpest disappointments of his life, the knowledge that the bones found beneath the red wall were almost certainly not those of Peter. His successor, John XXIII, held the chair for less than five years, dying on June 3, 1963. Within a week of this sad event, and well before the election of a new pope, a conversation took place in the Vatican between Professor Correnti and Dr. Guarducci. Lasting only a few casual moments, it would set in motion the final phase of the quest that had begun nearly a quarter century before.

The two scientists had known each other for some years. Occasionally, Dr. Guarducci had visited her friend in his Vatican workroom to inquire about progress on the bones. Their exchange this time (as Dr. Guarducci recalled it) was brief and offhand.

"You know," remarked Correnti, "it is very curious. In that little box of bones I have found the remains of only a single individual, and not of many, as in the first and second groups."

"A single individual?" Dr. Guarducci responded in some surprise. Along with many others, she had assumed that the box must hold the remains of several persons. "And have you established the sex?"

"Yes, masculine."

"And the age?"

"An advanced age. Between sixty and seventy years." Correnti paused, then added, "It is a man of robust constitution."

Explaining that all areas of the skeleton were present except for the feet, he said that judging by the soil still adhering to the bones, the body must first have been buried in the earth. Curiously, at some unknown time the bones had been enclosed in a wrapping of purple cloth—the bare bones, not the body itself. At the thought of the little mouse, its diminutive skeleton sharing the honors paid to the unknown man, both smiled in amusement. They parted for the day agreeing that it was indeed a singular circumstance that the human remains should prove to be those of one man.

Who could this have been, Dr. Guarducci found herself wondering, to have deserved burial so near Peter, actually within his shrine? From what lone grave had his decayed bones been lifted? To such questions the possible answers were nearly endless, involving a span of some thousand years, from the building of the graffiti wall in the third century right up to the Middle Ages. So, at least, it appeared to the scientist in those first hours after she learned the results of the testing. But a quiet spark had been struck, and her disciplined instincts now began to sift unbidden through a myriad of facts, guesses, and discarded theories.

During the evening after the conversation with Correnti, she continued to be mildly disturbed by some vague half-thought, a teasing echo of memory, which insisted on straying just out of reach. During the following day the feeling persisted, and the next morning as she prepared to leave her house for the university, there sounded dimly in her conscious mind, faintly reverberating, the two Greek words ΠΕΤΡΟΣ ΕΝΙ (Petros Eni).

Not for ten years had she given any thought to the inscription found by Ferrua inside the repository, scratched on the chunk of red plaster that had been shaken loose from the end-wall. While doing her original work on the mass of encoded graffiti, she had also taken a few days to study this isolated Peter graffito and had reached a conclusion satisfying to herself but which had not convinced everyone. The second word, the ENI, she had thought then, might be taken as complete in itself, rather than as the remaining portion of a longer word.

In ancient Greek, ENI (ENI) had sometimes been used, mostly in poetry, as a contraction of the verb ENEOTI, meaning "is within." The literal rendering of the red wall graffito would then be "Peter is within." But since, in this case, the word had a funerary context, its true reading could rightly be expanded to "Peter is buried in here."

At the time in 1953 when Dr. Guarducci first studied this inscription, no one among the experts had any doubt that, whatever its true meaning, the writing of it must have preceded the building of the graffiti wall. That the words had reference to the grave in the central chamber was a fact taken for granted. Some pious pilgrim of the late second century, kneeling in prayer, on the spur of the moment had hurriedly inscribed the two words, using some handy fine-pointed instrument (the cuts in the plaster are thin and shallow). Subsequently, the scratches had been covered up by the west end of the jutting graffiti wall. With this early assessment of the physical facts, Dr. Guarducci had fully agreed.

Now, two days after her talk with Professor Correnti, as she walked the busy corridors of the university, the phrase "Peter is buried in here," continued to whisper itself softly, insistently. At last the nagging question rose abruptly to the surface and, standing suddenly still, she almost recited it aloud: *Could* these graffiti wall bones be Peter's?

No, of course not, she instantly told herself. It made no sense at all. Why would Peter's bones be in the wall rather than where they belonged, in the central grave? If there had been the slightest chance of such a thing, how on earth could the four excavators have so completely missed it? And how could the placement of the Peter inscription be explained, sealed as it was inside the cavity where no one would ever notice it? Then there was the repository itself—everyone agreed that it had been opened in the Middle Ages, and who knew how many times it might have been violated before that?

But *had* the repository been opened? Why couldn't those tenth- or eleventh-century coins have gotten in by some sort of accident? The mouse! Surely if the marble cavity could be entered by a mouse, then the coins too might somehow have entered later, dropping in from above or at the sides. The official report had noted the roughness of the wall-fill above the repository, with its many cracks and fissures. The report had even explained that between the graffiti wall and the red wall a slight separation had developed because of settling. A great number of coins, nearly two thousand of them, had been found in and around the shrine, most dating from the Middle Ages. It would hardly be surprising if some of these had, suddenly or gradually, found their way down along the fissures or between the two wall surfaces.

Her mind now in a whirl, for the next two weeks Dr. Guarducci told her thoughts to no one as she feverishly evaluated every angle of the startling idea. How and when had the Peter graffito been written on the red wall, if that particular spot had been blocked? Of course! Through the front opening of the repository. After the bones had been laid in and just before the niche was walled up, at the last moment someone had reached in, probably with his left hand, and had made the hasty scratches, no doubt acting on impulse, moved by a vague wish to leave some definite identification.

But why, in the first place, had the bones been moved from the grave to the wall, and who was responsible? Constantine? And had he done it to preserve the relics forever from all threat of interference, especially vandalism? Perhaps it had also been thought necessary to lift them out of danger from floods, and the hazard posed by the drastic and constant drainage problem on the hill, as well as the excessively humid atmosphere beneath the soil.

Growing surer, she took Professor Correnti into her confidence, then her sister, and one or two trusted colleagues at the university. All were immediately intrigued by the theory, and offered encouragement, particularly Correnti, who suggested several tests that might be made and said he would be glad to help.

Concerning one thing, however, Dr. Guarducci remained troubled. When and how should she inform the Vatican authorities? Even by voicing her theory, she felt, she would be calling into serious question the competence of the original excavators, all men of high standing. But this minor dilemma was solved for her by an event that took place on June 21 1963. On that day an old friend of the Guarducci family, Cardinal Giovanni Battista Montini, was elected to the chair of Peter. She would wait, she decided, and present her ideas directly to Pope Paul VI.

The first chance for an audience with the busy new pope did not come until some four months later, in November 1963. Dr. Guarducci was to present him with copies of her own writings on the excavations, especially her latest work, which had already been translated into five languages. She would use this opportunity to reveal her secret, and ask permission to carry out the necessary tests.

Conducted to a small room adjacent to the Pope's private library, Dr. Guarducci found her volumes waiting her, placed neatly on a marble table. Shortly afterward, the Pope entered the room, greeted his guest, chatted in friendly fashion for a few moments, then accepted the gift of books, which he glanced through with unfeigned delight. The door of the room had been left ajar, and through it Dr. Guarducci could see people standing and passing, a situation which left her uneasy. For now at least, what she had to tell was for the Pope's ears alone. Sensing her discomfort, Paul crossed the room and closed the door. As he came back there was a quizzical look on his face.

The thought of what she was about to announce brought on an excited fluttering of the heart, and in a single sentence she made her statement. It was extremely probable, she said breathlessly, that the true relics of St. Peter, almost half of his skeleton, in fact, had been found and could be satisfactorily identified, if His Holiness would permit.

Taken unaware, Paul gave a little start, his eyes brightening in mixed surprise and pleasure. But he was obviously puzzled, and after assuring his guest of his joy at the news, he asked diplomatically who else knew about this unexpected development. Naming Correnti and one or two others, Dr. Guarducci briefly outlined the circumstances of the discovery. Certain tests would be needed, she finished, for which His Holiness' permission was required.

In the Pope's crowded schedule only a few minutes had been allowed for this meeting, and the time had now expired. He was about to make a Christmas pilgrimage to Jerusalem, he said, and preparations for this would occupy most of his time. But as soon as possible after his return he looked forward to a full discussion of the topic. It was a subject very close to his heart.

In two subsequent meetings with Pope Paul, in January and February 1964, at which Correnti was present along with the box of bones, and photographs of the repository, the new theory was thoroughly aired. The research needed, Dr. Guarducci explained, consisted principally of four strands: chemical analysis of the soil encrusted on the bones to determine whether it matched the soil in the central grave; analysis of the fabric found with the bones to determine its content and to see if the threads really were of true gold; examination of the animal bones to see if they fitted the probable types of the animals to be found in the area in the first century. Her final request she put forward hesitantly. They would also like to examine the ancient head of Peter, or more exactly its remaining portions, preserved in the reliquary over the Lateran altar.

After asking some penetrating questions, Paul took only a moment to consider. Permission was granted for all four tests. He required only that the work be pursued under the authority of the new administrator, Monsignor Principi, who would be instructed to offer all possible aid.

In spring and summer 1964, the various tests were conducted at the University of Rome by volunteers from among Dr. Guarducci's colleagues. The few animal bones quickly proved to be those of domesticated stock, mostly from goats with a number from horses and cows. Bones of these same animals had been found in the first two groups, along with pigs and sheep, just the sort of tame menagerie to be expected on the rural outskirts of Rome and in the vicinity of Nero's stables. The skeleton of the little mouse was confirmed as entire, and as coming from a single, immature individual of the species. The tiny bones were indeed all quite desiccated, as well as completely free from clinging soil.

The shreds of cloth provided an intriguing interval. Viewed under a powerful microscope, they were seen to be woven of wool threads, the weave corresponding with what was known of Roman techniques. The cloth had been dyed what appeared to be a shade of purple, now mostly lightened by age to a dark brownish red. The gold-appearing threads were indeed made of pure gold, manufactured in two different ways. The first method consisted of an unusually fine coating of gold laminate applied over wool. For the second, a core of linen or cotton had been sheathed with an initial covering of copper acetate, and atop this had been applied a very delicate plating of gold. The high skill and technical knowledge underlying the process—considering that it had been done as early as the third or fourth century —impressed the scientists as little short of marvelous.

Examination of the various soils—from the central grave, the courtyard, and the graffiti wall—took longest and was not completed until July. Particles of earth from all three locations were broken down chemically to their basic elements, then under a microscope the mineral and other components were identified and their relative quantities enumerated. At the conclusion of the study there was no doubt: the soil scraped from the bones made a perfect match with the soil in the central grave. Both were of the type called sandy marl, quite different from the blue clay or yellow sand which occurred generally in Rome, and which overlay much of Vatican Hill.

As it turned out, examination of the head from the Lateran was an experience at the same time both satisfying and sorely trying. While these relics played no essential part in the case being made on behalf of the other bones, their mere existence posed an irritating factor. For a thousand years, at least, the Lateran head had been accepted as the true remnant of Peter's skull. Among the graffiti wall bones, on the other hand, numerous fragments of another skull had been found. What was the connection between the two? Did one cancel out the other? If so, which, and in what manner? Or could the existence of the two be harmonized? If endless confusion and debate was to be avoided, an answer was imperative.

Paul's permission to examine the Lateran relic, however, had not been unconditional. Correnti, with whatever assistants he might choose to help him from other fields of science, was to be allowed full access to the relic, and would be given all the time he deemed necessary. The reliquary would be transported to the Vatican workroom, and he might perform on the bones whatever tests were desired (of course, short of inflicting damage). Complete notes were to be kept, and a full set of photographs made. But the report, whatever the conclusions, was not to be published by Correnti and his colleagues. The Vatican itself would decide when and under what circumstances the report should appear. Meantime, Correnti might state only general conclusions: his inspection of the Lateran relics did, or did not, raise a conflict with the other bones.

This condition, at first glance so well calculated to provoke suspicion, was really quite reasonable. The bones available for study from the Lateran were too few, by far, to permit a sure determination either of sex or age at death, even if expressed in as low a degree as presumable. And the varied history of Peter's relics, these and others, presented a vastly complicated tapestry, its threads reaching back to the earliest centuries along impossibly tangled and tenuous lines of tradition. An anthropological study, done on such inadequate materials (a few cranial fragments, a small part of the jawbone, a few vertebrae) could be no more than a first step toward a definitive answer. Premature publication in this regard might easily prejudice later findings.

For several months Correnti and his team were occupied with the Lateran bones. At the termination of this slow and careful study, their conclusion was absolute: nothing found in the reliquary interfered in any way, not in the slightest, with the claims made for the graffiti wall bones.

It was during these months of testing that Dr. Guarducci, to her great surprise yet considerable relief, at last discovered that the four original excavators had not, after all, overlooked the potential importance of the graffiti wall bones, incredibly dismissing them to the damp and darkness of an ordinary storeroom. In conversation with Father Kirschbaum, especially, and later in correspondence, it gradually became clear how, in reality, the four had been the innocent victims of a single devastating stroke of blind chance, all their good work marred by perhaps the most regrettable and egregious blunder in archaeological history.

At first, inevitably, the shock of this revelation, coming twelve years after the death of Monsignor Kaas, led one or another of the four to deny that any such horrendous mishap could have taken place. The wall repository had been found empty, absolutely empty, except for some minor debris, they insisted, repeating that it had been opened in the Middle Ages—and then were helpless to account for the wooden box and its contents. But a patient review of the excavation history of 1941–42, along with close questioning of Giovanni Segoni, established the truth. Even with that, Kirschbaum was the only one of the four able to bring himself to an immediate acceptance of the troubling facts. The other three, at first, disassociated themselves from the work, and continued for a while to defend the complete validity of their own efforts, eventually falling into a morose silence. Few cared to blame them for this attitude. Their anguish at having had all their eager hopes defeated by so bitterly mocking a denouement aroused only sympathy.

By now utterly convinced that the bones could only be those of Peter, Dr. Guarducci in the waning months of 1964 assembled the evidence. Since absolute proof was still lacking, and perhaps would never be found, conviction lay in the strength of circumstances. These must be put together link by link, drawing on all that had been learned since the start of the excavations some twenty-five years earlier:

1. The sumptuous marble housing erected by Constantine over the Tropaion was intended to preserve forever both the true original grave of Peter and his earthly remains.

2. Within the ancient shrine stood a low wall containing a marble-lined repository. This special niche was constructed at the time of Constantine and there was no proof that it had ever afterward been violated.

3. Enclosed in the repository were parts of a human skeleton from the body of an elderly man of robust build, a description which immediately suggests St. Peter. The central chamber itself, located some four or five feet below the repository, was found empty.

4. Soil adhering to the bones in the repository proved they had originally been interred in the earth. Chemical analysis proved that this soil exactly matched the soil in the original grave under the monument.

5. The bones in the repository had been wrapped in cloth of royal purple, a sure indication of the unusually high dignity accorded the man. Threads of gold in the cloth reinforced this impression, since the combination of purple and gold was a fact well attested from antiquity as indicating imperial honors.

6. An inscription within the repository, in Greek, declared "Peter is buried in here." Other inscriptions on the outside of the repository, in Latin, invoked his name in prayer.

7. Transfer of the bones from the grave to the repository had almost certainly been done to secure the relics' safety. This could be related to the problems of flooding and excessive moisture that had definitely been reported of the area as early as Pope Damasus in the fourth century. Also to be seriously considered was the problem of vandalism growing out of religious bigotry, not negligible in that more violent age. The repository in the sturdy little wall had guarded against all such intrusions by permanently enclosing the precious remains on all sides.

8. The off-center location of the repository in relation to the shrine, a fact disturbing to some, was misleading to a hurried perusal. In reality the repository was an integral part of the marble housing, which simultaneously enclosed Peter's original grave, his earliest monument, the Tropaion, and his revered bones. And over this rich housing the vast basilica itself had been erected. In any case, the distance off-center was less than two feet, hardly significant when compared to the size of shrine and basilica.

By the end of 1964 the manuscript of the book in which Dr. Guarducci would reveal her secret, to both the general public and the scholarly world, was nearly ready for the press. Half the book was her own account, giving background and detail, and boldly setting forth the claim that the graffiti wall bones were Peter's. The second half of the book consisted of elaborate scientific reports supported by photographs, prepared by Correnti and the other scientists involved in the testing. The book was to be issued by the Vatican's own publishing house, Libreria Editrice Vaticana. While this affiliation at least implied some degree of official approval, there was to be no announcement to that effect. The arresting new theory would be allowed to make its own way through the rough shoals of scholarly review.

As a final bow in the direction of scientific rigor, all the working materials on which the theory was based had been submitted separately to five disinterested scholars. Three were respected archaeologists, two were language experts. All five, independently, gave their judgment that the procedures, and the conclusions from the evidence, were impeccable.

II

Decision

Accustomed to the polite, ordinarily placid atmosphere that usually surrounds scholarly debate, Dr. Guarducci was not prepared for the pained outcry that in many quarters greeted publication of her book in February 1965. Almost angrily, nonplussed scholars listed what they considered serious defects in her theory, both generally and in detail. Most damningly, it was charged, she had utterly failed to make plausible the rather astounding, if not downright ridiculous, claim regarding the provenance of Peter's supposed relics: found, lost, found again, put aside once more, then finally identified only through the merest chance. Her brief, strangely awkward exposition of that lengthy and astonishing episode, it was said, would leave even the most naïve of readers coldly unimpressed. And on top of this, she displayed an annoying tendency to push her evidence too far, offering as certain, things which were no more than probable or possible, if that.

There was justice in these charges. Rather incredibly, in her account Dr. Guarducci had told as little as possible about the background to the discovery. Instead, she contented herself with stating, in effect, that the bones had been removed by Monsignor Kaas in ignorance of their true identity and without the knowledge of the excavators, and that ten years later she had been able, as she expressed it, to "trace" them, but omitting all explanation of how the tracing was done. Then after still another decade, she said, following Correnti's work, she had "recognized" the possibility that they might be Peter's remains. No reason was offered for Kaas' high-handed actions, or for the excavators' ignorance, nor was anything said about Segoni's part in the little drama. The bald statement, made still less convincing by a labored exposition, was woefully inadequate to its task.

The failure was unfortunate, and was to cause no end of misunderstanding (echoes of which still sound today). But it did not flow from scholarly deficiency. Largely, it was an error of the heart. A misguided wish to shield the reputations of all concerned had clouded the scientist's usual good sense, leading her to try the impossible—gaining acceptance for the relics while telling less than the full truth.

Problematic enough was the unprecedented reality of the situation. Now in the public mind the difficulties had been redoubled, leading a few critics to dismiss the whole, fantastic episode as the fevered result of one overenthusiastic scholar's relentless effort to "find" Peter's relics. From the very first, it was said, she had set out determined to discover the bones of the apostle—so of course she *had* discovered them. Too late, Dr. Guarducci realized her mistake.

Aside from that major flaw, there were several other objections from the critics which also struck home. But these were susceptible of direct proof, and Dr. Guarducci quickly moved to close the gaps.

The first concerned the purple cloth. As all the critics agreed, this royal wrapping was a very telling point in the theory's favor, definitely associating the bones with a dignity far above the ordinary, even implying some sort of ultimate significance. Yet Dr. Guarducci's treatment of this critical point was sadly incomplete. How could anyone be certain that the cloth had in fact originally been true Roman purple, if it now appeared mostly a deep, rusty red? It was not sufficient, rather it was thoroughly unscientific, simply to assume that this present color was the faded reflection of an original vibrant purple.

For that matter, exactly what shade had the ancients taken to be purple? Some experts, citing wall paintings and mosaics, insisted that violet or mauve was closer to Roman purple than was the modern conception, and that Roman purple did not have a red base. It was also claimed that ordinary wool was never used by the Romans to make purple fabrics, and in any case imitation purple, reddish in tint, was not unknown among wealthy Roman citizens desirous of aping their betters. Very clever things could be done with vegetable dyes, particularly cochineal, achieving a purplish effect without quite encroaching on the royal privilege.

These objections were not frivolous, and the whole arcane subject of ancient textile coloring now threatened to submerge discussion of the repository cloth, sinking it into a rambling, many-sided disagreement. As it happened, a little-known branch of archaeology was soon able, again through chemistry, to supply a definitive answer.

The Roman purpling agent, experts had long known, was a very special dye kept firmly under state control. More recently the source of the dye had been found: it was made from an extract of Mediterranean shellfish, *murex brandaris* or *murex trunculus,* one giving a slightly deeper tone than the other. A test for identifying this shellfish dye had been developed which was both simple and admittedly infallible. The object to be tested was first treated with hydrochloric acid. If the color, even though faded, was the true Roman purple derived from the shellfish, it would be unchanged in hue, though a little heightened. The same object was then treated with hydrosulfite of ammonia. Slowly the color would turn to a muddy yellow, then on exposure to the air would gradually resume its original red, greatly intensified. With this test, the reaction of any dye except that made from the *murex* would be radically different.

In a laboratory at the University of Rome, Dr. Guarducci and a colleague from the chemistry department prepared several threads taken from the repository fabric. Under the microscope, to Dr. Guarducci's eye they appeared a dull, dark red. When a drop of hydrochloric acid was applied, the color held fast, only brightening a little. Then the hydrosulfite was dropped onto the slide while the scientist watched apprehensively. After a few seconds she reported with a sigh of relief that the threads had begun blossoming in yellow. Exposed to the air, they were again put under the microscope. The yellow had entirely disappeared and the threads uniformly glowed a brilliant deep red.

For some critics, an even stronger objection than the question of purple concerned the repository itself, and it was twofold. First, they claimed, it was very far from being proved that the repository had remained unopened through the sixteen centuries since Constantine. In fact, what evidence there was tended to support the excavators' belief that someone in the Middle Ages had broken into it from the narrow east end. The casual citing of overhead fissures, and a wall separation, through which the medieval coins *might* have entered, was hardly convincing without some supporting evidence. (The mouse was wryly set aside as being an unreliable witness.)

Second, it was not at all clear why Dr. Guarducci should insist that the repository had been built by Constantine to be part of his marble memorial. From what could be seen by others, the cavity might have been hollowed out at any time during the century before that, simultaneously with the building of the graffiti wall itself. So long as these two crucial questions remained open, the critics insisted with strict logic, the argument for Peter's bones could hardly be judged unshakable.

Accompanied by several archaeologists, all of them well versed in ancient building techniques, Dr. Guarducci entered the cramped chamber before the graffiti wall. Permission to dismantle the repository, in order to make an exhaustive examination of the oblong cavity, had willingly been granted by the Pope. The study could be made without inflicting harm or loss, the scientists had assured him, and would establish beyond doubt whether the repository had ever been breached.

First, the marble slab at the east end was removed, baring the inside brickwork of the wall's outer shell. The slab at the opposite end was also taken out, and the larger bottom slab, its size preventing removal, was then turned up on its long edge and

25. Dr. Margherita Guarducci in her study about 1960. What seemed an impossible challenge, aided by an accidental find, led her to the ultimate discovery.

25A. The wooden box in which lay the human skeletal remains taken from the repository in the graffiti wall. It was overlooked for some ten years, and only an accident of fate led to its recovery.

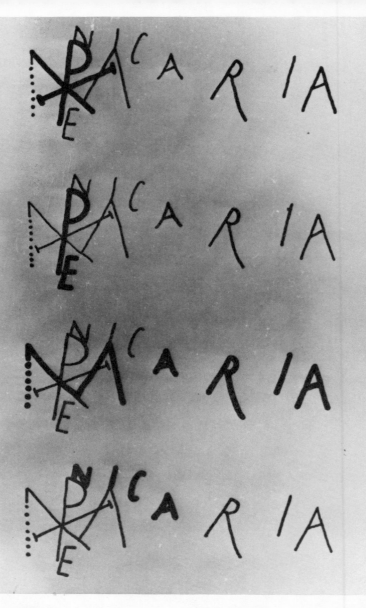

26.   Sketch of an inscription from the graffiti wall, redrawn to show its four phases. 1) the *chi-rho* symbol for Christ( ); 2) an E is added to the bottom of the *rho* (Greek R) which here is employed as a Latin P, giving a reference to Peter; 3) part of the *chi-rho* is used to make an M and the letters ARIA added, for Mary; 4) the first A of *Maria* is used as the termination of NICA (Greek *NIKA* for *victory*).

27. The chunk of plaster from the red wall, found by Antonio Ferrua in the marble repository. Shallow but definite scratches spell out in Greek the words *Petr[os]eni*, which some interpret as *Peter is buried in here*.

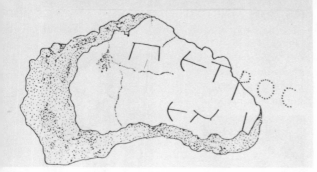

27A. The interior of the marble-lined repository hidden in the graffiti wall. The brickwork at the far end was proved to be the work of Roman masons, and to have stood untouched since the recess was originally built in the mid third century.

a

28. Here and on the following two pages are shown some of the skeletal remains identified as St. Peter's.
a. Fragment from the skull (cranium).
b. Fragment from the left shoulder (clavicle).
c. Fragments from the left forearm (ulna).
d. Fragment from the right arm (humerus).

b

c

d

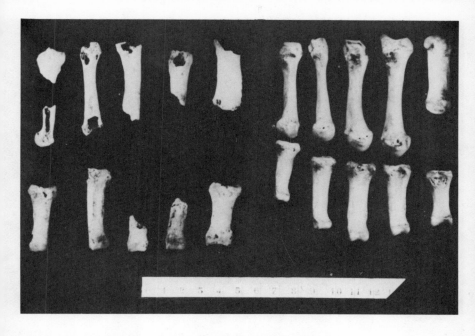

29. a. Finger bones and metacarpals from the left hand.
    b. Fragments of the pelvis and sacrum.

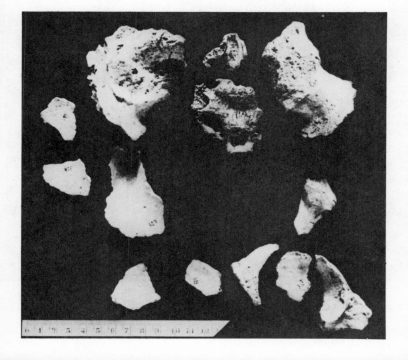

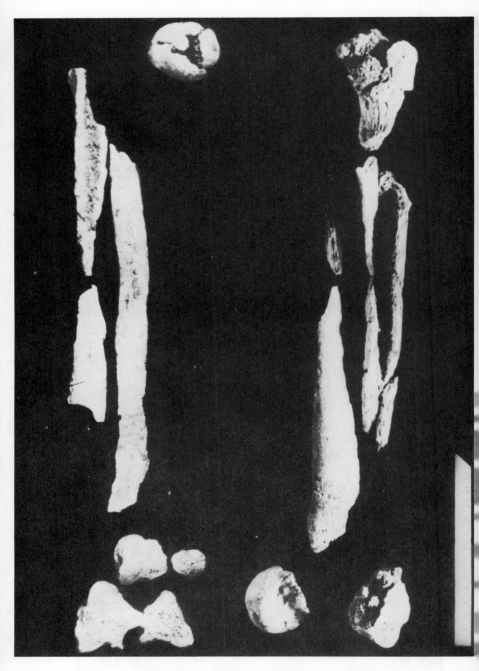

30.   Fragments of the right and left thighs (femur).

31. In 1968, encased in special boxes of heavy plastic, the bones of St. Peter were returned to the repository in the graffiti wall, where they had lain undisturbed for some sixteen hundred years.

32. Today, bronze grillwork doors close off access to Peter's shrine and grave beneath the basilica's high altar. The area is still essentially unaltered except for the minor changes wrought by the excavators.

rested against the rear wall. With this, the man moving the slabs reported that he could see several coins in the crevasses between the slabs. Handed out, they proved to be similar to those found previously. Almost certainly, they were all medieval.

With a floodlight illuminating the cavity's interior, the experts probed and measured on every side, paying special attention to the wall at the east end. This narrow section contained bricks of slightly varied lengths and thicknesses, the coloration ranging from reddish to dull ocher. Beyond doubt, this was Roman work. The layering of the bricks, their placement, and the mortaring between them were unmistakable. And absolutely no slightest trace of tampering could be seen, no chisel marks, no indications of rebuilding in the mortar. The east wall had never been interfered with since its first construction. Since there could have been no access from any other side, nor from above or below, it was now certain that the repository had existed untouched from the start. But when, exactly, had that been?

Study of the wall-fill (a hard jumble of mortar, brick, and stone which had been shoveled down into the hollow outer shell as it rose under the builder's hand) yielded a convincing answer. The oblong space had definitely been scooped out of a solid entity, when the wall was already standing. So much was abundantly clear from a close look at the fill above the cavity and below the bottom slab. That the work had been done in Constantine's era was just as obvious. In several spots, the blue-white plaster covering the face of the graffiti wall had been carried over to cover some small breaks in the red wall, breaks which had occurred during the building of the shrine.

Only a day was needed for this investigation, and the decision was firm: whatever had been found in the repository at its opening in 1942 had definitely lain there, undisturbed, since closure of the housing shrine by Constantine's workmen in the early fourth century. The medieval coins must have worked their way down, most probably over some considerable period of time, through the fissures and probably also through the separation between the two walls. A likely precipitating force, for most of them, was the general disturbance caused in the area when the

Callixtus altar was installed in the twelfth century. A great deal of jarring must have occurred with these ponderous operations, a massive disturbance which could easily have sent some of the many coins tumbling down. Most, of course, would have been of recent medieval vintage.

To a large degree, this hypothesis was later confirmed. One of the two coins recovered from the wooden box, it was found, was not medieval, but dated to fourth-century Rome. It contained the image and motto of the Emperor Constantius II, nephew of Constantine, and had been minted about the year 357. At that time, the repository had already been sealed for perhaps three decades. This Constantius coin could have entered the repository only by slipping along some crack.

Quite a number of the critics had also decried the omission from the testing of radiocarbon dating, a procedure which could fix the absolute age of the bones. The reply to this suggestion was given by Professor Correnti: since the bones had definitely lain in the cavity since the early fourth century, they were already proved to be of an age within 250 years or so of Peter's death. Carbon dating, which carried a plus-or-minus factor, could do no better than this. Also, for such testing, a portion of a bone would have to be destroyed, and this sacrifice no one was willing to make, particularly when it would yield only corroboration, not pioneer data.

Inevitably, it was also asked why the bones could not be the remains of some other high church dignitary of the early period. There seemed no positive reason, among all the evidence presented, why these bones unequivocally had to be Peter's. This was an ingenuous position, attainable only by abruptly setting aside the inescapable conclusions from all the circumstances. As Dr. Guarducci realized, a full answer would need a rehearsal of the entire excavation history from start to finish. Still, a short reply was possible: if these were not the bones of Peter, but of some other unknown official, totally ignored by history, it was more than strange that no slightest identification was given. Further, it would be inexplicable to have another person, of whatever rank, buried in the tomb acknowledged to be the apostle's.

Rather than casual guesswork, science dealt with the hard evidence at hand. In this instance, the evidence left no room for the introduction of a mysterious stranger.

Vastly more troubling to many people than these relatively minor points was the notion that Constantine would have moved the relics at all from their first resting place in the central chamber, the original bare grave. The reasons given by Dr. Guarducci for this move—rather blithely advanced, said her critics—were quite inadequate, much the weakest part of her case. It need only be recalled, they insisted, that the enormous basilica itself had been constructed over this immensely difficult terrain precisely because the grave and the relics could *not* be moved, a rigid tradition prohibiting it. Two feet, ten feet, or a hundred feet, the distance moved was not the crucial factor.

And, the critics inquired, did enclosure of the bones in the graffiti wall really accomplish anything which could not have been achieved equally as well, or even better, by new construction in and over the central grave, using concrete, bronze, lead, or any material desired? Surely Constantine's capable engineers could have devised some arrangement to guard the bones in the original grave against floods, humidity, vandalism, and every other hazard that might threaten them.

Further, the repository itself, despite the lining of marble slabs, was nothing but a miserable hole in a nondescript wall. Was this poor, makeshift cavity the best that Constantine could do for the precious remains, when he had lavished so much effort and expense on the richly decorated housing shrine and the magnificent basilica towering over it? For any logical mind, sensitive to the fitness of things, the disparity was glaring.

For these arguments, Dr. Guarducci had no new answers. Patiently, she repeated that all the circumstances, taken together, did undoubtedly support the authenticity of the bones, and their removal from central grave to marble repository was simply a fact that must be accepted. For her and others, the reasons cited, relating to security and preservation from moisture, were sufficient. But in her view, she insisted, the difficulty was not really so serious as some critics would make it appear. The bones, whether resting in the wall or in the original grave, made an integral part of the true shrine. Within its marble-and-porphyry walls there was gathered, at once, all that pertained to Peter's burial—the grave, the Tropaion, and his surviving remains. Such was the physical fact. If transfer of the bones offended modern ideas, perhaps that reaction only heightened the changes to be expected in human attitudes over the course of sixteen centuries.

In July 1967 a pamphlet was published containing Dr. Guarducci's extended reply to her critics. No longer in a protective mood, she unsparingly revealed the full details of Monsignor Kaas' silent interference, as well as her own accidental discovery of the bones through Segoni—whose notarized affidavit, she made sure to mention, was on permanent file in the Vatican. Now firmly convinced of the theory's truth, she had no patience with any critic whose grasp of the facts was less than sure, or whose interpretations relied too heavily on hypothetical groping. In rather abrupt style, she covered all the major and minor objections, point by point, not always avoiding a certain sharpness of tone in citing what she conceived to be outright errors.

For fifteen sometimes weary years, Dr. Guarducci had not been free of the question of Peter's burial, and much of her work had met strong initial skepticism from people she considered unqualified to pass on it. Now, she felt, the task was completed once and for all, with no smallest murmur of dissent overlooked. The bodily remains of St. Peter, rescued from the oblivion of centuries and from the fumbling of human hands, might at last rest in peace.

Crowded in and around the small chamber in which stood the graffiti wall were some dozen clergymen, most wearing ceremonial vestments. At their head, in miter and cope, was Pope Paul. Standing nearest the wall were Monsignor Principi and Professor Correnti. Beside these two, her head veiled in black, was Margherita Guarducci. It was June 27, 1968. The day before, the Pope had made his electrifying announcement to the world that the skeletal remains of St. Peter, Prince of Apostles, had been identified. Now the bones were to be returned to their ancient resting place. By order of the Pope, the ceremony would be brief.

On a table nearby lay nineteen boxes, variously shaped, all made of heavy, transparent plexiglass. In each box, resting on white foam rubber, were one or more bones, separated according to the parts of the body: head, arms, hands, vertebrae, ribs, trunk, pelvis, legs. Attached to each box was an identifying label. Two of the boxes contained the animal bones, including those of the mouse, which were also to be restored to the repository. The repository's entire contents were to be left just as they had been found, to the last detail.

Professor Correnti moved up to the low opening in the wall. As the boxes were handed to him by Dr. Guarducci and Monsignor Principi, he placed them in the cavity according to a prearranged sequence. When all had been entered, a glass front was fixed in place. A prayer was then recited, after which a notary read out a description of the proceedings, later to be entered in the Vatican's permanent records.

Led by the Pope, the party filed out of the chamber as an attendant slowly swung shut on the graffiti wall a heavy gate made of ornate open-work bronze. Through its bars could be seen the floodlit, glassed-in repository, less than five feet away. Visible just inside the rim of the opening were two boxes. In one lay the largest and best preserved of the bones, the left tibia. In the other were the single tooth and the twenty-nine fragments of the skull.

12

The Ancient Silence

If the critics were right, if it was not Constantine who had Peter's bones removed from the central grave, wrapped in purple cloth, and deposited in the graffiti wall, then one thing is clear: the transfer must have taken place before the Emperor's dramatic arrival on the scene. But who, in that case, did order the removal? And when was it done and for what possible reason? Instinct whispers that the answers to those tantalizing questions may well provide the key to much that is still, more than a dozen years after Pope Paul's announcement, at odds in the history of the relics.

Doubts about the grateful Emperor having arranged the transfer are not only legitimate, they are inescapable. The enormous physical effort that was expended in erecting the original basilica—oriented over one exact spot upon ruggedly uneven terrain—was necessary precisely because the intended focal point, the bones, could *not* be moved. This unarguable fact really leaves no room at all for the claim that, just prior to the start of work on the basilica, the focal point *was* moved. Nor has a convincing reply been made to those critics who instinctively shake their heads in stubborn disbelief at the idea that the revered bones could have been stored, officially and perma-

nently, in such a drab cavity, bare of all formal indication that
the Prince of the Apostles lay within.

With full justice, then, it may be concluded that the transfer
of Peter's bones was accomplished sometime in the half century
or so before the advent of Constantine—that is, in the interval
between completion of the graffiti wall, about 250–60, and the
start of work on the shrine, about 315. To uncover the reason for
the transfer, and if possible to identify those responsible, it will
be best to pass over those fifty years and go back to the beginning, to the day of Peter's death. What was there about the
burial that might later have prompted anyone to think of moving the remains?

Strangely overlooked in all that has been written about the
apostle's grave is a single fact, fairly obvious in the circumstances, which now assumes some major importance. All the evidence shows that, right from the start, Peter's burial was and
remained a *hidden* one. Until the day when the gravesite was
revealed to Constantine, so that he might crown it with a basilica, its true location was one of the Christian community's most
carefully guarded secrets. The proof of that, while not direct or
abundant, is more than adequate—even without the natural in-
ference to be made from a knowledge of those troubled times.

Under Roman law Peter was an executed criminal, put to
death as an enemy of the state. As a result, his body was not entitled to proper burial, nor did his relatives or friends have the
right to recover it. The corpse of such a despised individual,
most often, would have been flung scornfully into the Tiber, in-
cinerated on the city dump, or thrown out for animals to devour.
Thus after Peter's body had been recovered—either by stealth or
by bribery, the only two possibilities open—his burial consti-
tuted a seriously illegal action. If located by the authorities the
grave could lawfully be despoiled, and the corpse, or what
remained of it, destroyed. Rome's Christians, faced with this
very real threat, fervent in their wish to preserve the mortal part
of Christ's first Vicar on earth, must very soon have formed a
conspiracy of silence regarding Peter's last resting place.

So much is conjecture—legitimate enough, but still conjecture.

There are, however, four items of hard evidence which can be offered in support.

The first concerns a tradition found in the writings of the Emperor Julian, a nephew of Constantine, who would have had ample opportunity to test its truth. Flatly, even if offhandedly, Julian states that in the last decade of the first century—that is, some twenty or thirty years after Peter's martyrdom—the apostle's grave was already being venerated, and he adds, "secretly, it is true." That phrase, in that context, can only mean that the actual location of the grave itself was kept hidden.

The second and third items are really one, and concern certain puzzling facts turned up in the excavations, the full import of which has so far been ignored. They are best presented as questions: How can the unusual design of the Tropaion, its largely pagan derivation, be explained? And how does it happen that the name of Peter is never once written out *in full* among the crowding inscriptions on the graffiti wall, while in its coded form it appears as many as two dozen times?

Concerning the Tropaion's design, only one answer will satisfy. The close similarity to pagan architecture, and the total lack of any Christian element were no accidents. The form was deliberately chosen, and therefore could only have been meant as a disguise, a means of hiding the monument's real function. Probably the two upper niches once held urns, or statues of a neutral sort, in further imitation of pagan practice. No wandering visitor, pausing to view the site, would have had any cause to suspect the presence of the outlawed faith.

The absence of Peter's full name on the graffiti wall must also be explained primarily as the result of a wish for concealment. Clearly, the avoidance of the full name could only have resulted from an absolute prohibition, laid down by the church authorities. Without this prohibition, strictly maintained, surely one pilgrim at least, perhaps two or three or more, would not have bothered with symbols, but would have freely and unconcernedly scratched down all five letters of Peter's name. The use of mystical cryptography, it must be remembered, was at all times informal, very much dependent on individual impulse.

Where every occurrence of Peter's name, without exception, is found in code, some controlling factor is needed to account for the unnatural consistency. Access to the monument would certainly not have been unrestricted, and the ban on Peter's full name was undoubtedly enforced by an official on the site.

The fourth item, for some minds, offers the most convincing evidence of all, especially when judged against the background of the first three. No longer can it be taken as a mere accident of history that throughout the whole range of ancient Christian literature (first to early fourth centuries) there is little but silence regarding Peter's death and burial, no dependable description of his crucifixion, no reliable hint as to the precise location of his grave, no slightest reference to his monument. (The mention of the Tropaion by Gaius occurs in a private letter.) This massive silence regarding the most important personage in the early church definitely bespeaks concerted action.

Of course, Peter is mentioned repeatedly in these early documents, but always in a general way, the references glancing and allusive. Often the text breaks off, changes direction, at the very point where it would be natural to have some pointed reference to his martyrdom, to the fact that his venerated remains were still preserved at Rome. But there is nothing, and a widespread conspiracy of silence, long continued, does not appear so extreme an idea to account for the remarkable oversight. In those trying times, no Christian would have needed much persuasion to agree that in the body of St. Peter the church possessed one of its most precious treasures, worth any effort to safeguard.

Preservation of Peter's remains, then, was at all stages the paramount aim. That being so, and since it is now agreed that the graffiti wall was erected during the mid third century, the enigma of the marble cavity appears ready to yield.

During the decade 250–60, under four different emperors, but principally Valerian, successive persecutions raged through the Empire, naturally fiercest in the city of Rome. In that time of great hazard, transfer of the bones from the grave to the concealed repository would have been almost a necessity. Besides the danger of accidental discovery, growing out of the prevalent tension and chaos, there was always the chance that, under torture or in a pitiful effort at survival, some unfortunate believer might have been tempted to barter away the secret of the bones. Such defections did occur, of course, often with melancholy effects for others, and one of the early church's most vexing problems was to decide how these people, when repentant, should be dealt with. Nor is it without relevance that when Valerian's persecution began it focused first on Christian cemeteries, an imperial decree forbidding all access to them for either visiting or burial.

But the bones certainly would not have remained in the graffiti wall from Valerian's time on. The makeshift construction of the repository decisively marks it as a hurried operation, begun perhaps at a moment's notice, never meant to be permanent. When the danger had definitely subsided—perhaps about 270—the bones would have been returned to their proper station in the earth. The empty repository, however, would not have been forgotten. Once having served as a secure hiding place, it would naturally be employed a second time when danger threatened. The removal of a little plaster and some sort of inner lining, insertion of the purple-wrapped bones, then replacement of lining and plaster and the painting of an innocuous design on the exterior surface, would all have been the work of an hour or less.

Thus, decades later, when Diocletian's Empire-wide persecution fell with such unparalleled savagery, it became a later generation's urgent duty once again to conceal the bones. And there in the cavity they lay, safe from all who could wish them harm, through the opening years of the fourth century. With the advent of the friendly Constantine, an event totally unforeseen and unpredictable, the bones happened still to be in the wall.

Several years passed after Constantine's victorious entry into Rome at the head of his troops before the reigning Pope, Sylvester, revealed to him the true location of Peter's grave. The Emperor then proceeded to erect over it, at Sylvester's own suggestion, the marble-and-porphyry shrine, and the towering basilica. So much is historical fact. Implied in all of this, taken wholly for granted, is the underlying assumption that in disclosing the site of the grave, Pope Sylvester must also have told the truth about the location of the bones. But that conclusion, given the theory of a hidden grave, is the least likely of all. Too well would Sylvester have understood the pressing danger in a society whose every nuance of life was ruled by imperial decree, most particularly in matters of religion. When he led Constantine to the Tropaion, identifying it as Peter's, the bones were not lying in the central chamber but in the graffiti wall, and *that* fact the cautious Pope certainly would not have revealed. The belief that he did so arises from a distortion in historical perspective.

The great event in Christian history, the revolution in freedom wrought by Constantine, is too often telescoped by writers into a single momentous instant, sharply dividing the three centuries which preceded from the sixteen which followed. But for the people of the time, that was not the way it happened. In reality, that victorious instant stretched over a long, anxious period in which apprehensive Christians, scarcely allowing themselves to believe in the miracle, waited to see whether, this time, Rome's hard pagan heart had truly softened. All were only too aware that the Emperor's edict granting them liberty of worship could not in itself guarantee the future. They knew this not only by well-sharpened instinct, but from experience.

Constantine was not the first to try giving freedom to Christians. Fifty years before, the pagan Gallienus had also granted them toleration, lifting the criminal status which had been in force since Nero. Gallienus had even asked Christians to offer prayers to their god for his own welfare. He soon died, however, and his decree was quickly set aside. Thereafter, Christians once more went in fear of their lives. In the year 311, shortly before the victory of Constantine, still another emperor, Galerius, renewed the promise of freedom when he halted the persecution begun by Diocletian: from then on Christianity was to be accepted by the state. But that promise, too, had soon been snatched away.

Remembering these earlier false dawns, aware that in Rome

the course of events could alter with chilling swiftness, Pope Sylvester would certainly have been slow in giving up the 250-year-old tradition of secrecy which surrounded the location of the bones. The site of the grave itself he could reveal—in the altered conditions it would have been hard to conceal for long—but exact knowledge of the precious bones could await a surer day, when the passage of time had proved the real strength of Constantine's new beliefs. The most convincing sign of the Emperor's conversion would have been baptism. But this act of humility and submission he showed no inclination to accept.

And in Sylvester's fateful decision not to give up the secret, there resides the solution to yet another of the riddles posed by the excavations, a riddle which still troubles all who stand before the Niche of the Pallia puzzling over its oddly lopsided appearance. Here, finally, is the one reason which adequately explains why the interfering bulk of the graffiti wall was allowed to remain in place, why it was not promptly removed in order to restore the Tropaion's original balanced design. It was a simple case of necessity: with Peter's bones hidden in the wall's interior, a fact which was not to be disclosed, the Pope had no choice but to retain it. Control of all details concerned with enshrinement of the Tropaion lay within the papal power, and any reason Sylvester gave for keeping the wall in place must have been received as final by the Emperor's architects.

In ignorance of the truth about the bones, Constantine may have ordered Peter's grave opened, as some documents state, and as it seems probable that he did. If so, what would he have seen? Assuredly, the church had anticipated this move, and Constantine would certainly have discovered a set of bones lying in the central grave. But they would not have been Peter's. Whose then? Quite probably, the Emperor's wondering eyes beheld the very same bones which, sixteen centuries later, were to be discovered by Kirschbaum beneath the red wall. And it is possible to go one step further.

If Peter's illegal burial was hurried, perhaps carried out at night, and was to be a secret, then his body may have been purposely interred in an existing grave, one already occupied. In the circumstances, no better concealment could have been wished. In that case, Peter's unknown companions in death, very likely other Christian martyrs, can be said to have served their chief well, for even their few pitiful bones played a part in the conspiracy of silence. The remains found under the red wall, which today lie neglected in the Vatican, may be worthy of more honor than anyone has yet understood.

Two last questions remain: Why didn't Pope Sylvester, or his successors, tell Constantine the truth about the bones at some later time, when it became evident that the new freedom of worship was indeed to be permanent? And how and why was it that all knowledge of them became lost? The answers, once again, arise easily out of the theory of a hidden grave.

After starting construction on the basilica, Constantine reigned for another two decades, mostly from his splendid new capital at Constantinople. But these were burdensome years, full of turmoil and confusion, with church and state groping toward a common understanding in many areas (was the Emperor to be *in* the church or *over* it?). And matters were further complicated by the disturbing fact that paganism, also by edict of the Emperor, was still flourishing, still openly antagonistic to its rival. In these circumstances, twenty years could not have seemed long to the Pope and his harried ministers. During all that time, moreover, Constantine continued to refuse baptism. Only on his deathbed did he submit.

Constantine died in the year 337. His immediate successors were all weak men, vacillating, unsure of themselves and their ideas about the church, some even embracing one or another of the early heresies. There could have been little inducement in these years for the church to risk a revelation about the bones. Then suddenly, shockingly, in the spring of the year 361, the worst fears of the Christian community were starkly realized. Once more an avowed pagan ascended the throne.

The Emperor Julian, ever since known to Christians as the Apostate, was a man of learning and intelligence, but one with little use for toleration. From youth he had been under the shadowy spell of the old pagan mystery religions, had quietly nur-

tured a hatred of what he called "the fabrication of the Galileans
. . . composed by wickedness." For him, the Resurrection was "a
monstrous tale." Once in power, he moved rapidly to restore
pagan worship to its former preeminence, and for two long, dark
years he inexorably rolled back the gains that had been made by
the church. Passing laws that disenfranchised Christians in favor
of pagans, he also wrote and published tracts against Christianity. Ominously for Peter's bones, in one tract he declared his
abhorrence of the Christian habit of venerating certain of their
dead. "You have filled the whole world with tombs and sepul-
chers," he burst out accusingly, "and yet in your Scriptures it is
nowhere said that you must grovel among tombs and pay them
honor." Acting on that feeling, in one instance he even went so
far as to desecrate the grave of a Christian saint.

For a while in the mid-fourth century it seemed that the old
gods must certainly triumph, and that Christians would be
forced back into their former furtive existence. But this last
major threat was also destined to pass. Just when it appeared
that the Christian movement was under fatal attack, the most serious it had faced in many decades, Julian received a mortal
wound while leading his troops in battle. Lying on his deathbed,
foreseeing that the struggle against the followers of Christ was
lost, his final words were bitter: "Galilean, you have conquered!"

Some fifty years had intervened between the start of Constantine's reign and that of Julian, years in which the practice of
Christianity had been officially encouraged. Yet even that
lengthy period had not sufficed to guarantee its existence. At the
whim of a single man, it seemed, the whole widespread network
of Christianity, by then planted in most of the civilized world,
could still be hampered, outlawed, condemned. After Julian, and
probably for several decades, no pope would have thought
seriously of removing the bones from the safety of the graffiti
wall in order to return them to the earth of the central chamber.

At Julian's death in 363, Peter's bones had lain encased in the
marble repository for about sixty years. Succeeding popes wisely
allowed them to remain there, so that by the time Christianity
had at last become secure—perhaps soon after the year 400—the

secret of the bones must have grown hazy indeed, even in the church's inner circles. All were satisfied, however, that the bones did undoubtedly lie somewhere beneath the high altar. That they might not be arranged precisely and geometrically beneath the altar's center was something which came to matter less and less, until the day arrived when it ceased to matter at all.

If a time is to be named by which it may be said that the secret had been entirely forgotten, then the year 595 will do as well as any. In that year Pope Gregory the Great began the first large-scale alteration of the upper shrine and the high altar. His operations show no knowledge whatever of the true location of Peter's relics.

In the discussion so far, based on the theory of a hidden grave, it must be admitted that there lurks a difficulty, or an apparent difficulty. If the location of the grave was always to be kept a secret, then why did the church erect over it a conspicuous monument, the Tropaion, surrounded by other substantial structures? Even though disguised, all this hardly added to the grave's concealment. The seeming contradiction when resolved, however, leads straight to the discovery of what may be called the real secret of Peter's grave.

The evident reason why the church should have built atop the grave concerns the period in which the work was done. The mid second century was a time of fast-rising hope for Christians, and the hope, as it then appeared, was justified. Since the death of the Emperor Domitian, in A.D. 98, no official persecutions had scarred the land, no wholesale bloodletting had raged abroad. The laws against Christians, it is true, were still in force, and here and there in isolated flare-ups of local antagonism, Christians had continued to suffer and sometimes even die for their faith. But through most of this century the imperial throne was occupied by men of some intellectual stature, even social enlightenment (Nerva, Trajan, Hadrian, Antoninus Pius, Marcus Aurelius). All concentrated their attentions on enhancing the good order and prosperity of a society which was reaching toward unparalleled heights of civilized life. Active, organized

suppression of a religious minority living within the Empire had
no place in their scheme of rule.

Trajan, in a letter of the year 112 to a provincial governor, sets
the tone. Replying to a request for information on the procedure
to be used against Christians who were actually brought before
the court, he says that for admitted Christians there must be
punishment, but he also counsels moderation: "It is not possible
to lay down general rules for all such cases. Do not go out of
your way to look for them . . . where the party denies he is a
Christian, and shall make it evident that he is not by invoking
our gods, let him (notwithstanding any former suspicions) be
pardoned upon his repentance. Anonymous informations ought
not to be received in any sort of prosecution. It is introducing a
very dangerous precedent, and is quite foreign to the spirit of
our age."

This somewhat calmer view prevailed generally, and by the
time the red wall complex was built, at about mid-century, the
imperial power had passed to the responsible hands of the man
who is now often credited with being the most enlightened of all
Rome's emperors, Antoninus Pius (he was accorded the title
Pius precisely as a compliment to his personal character). The
red wall complex, in other words, was erected during the very
zenith of Rome's golden age, a period which thrillingly promised, or seemed to promise, a new day for Christianity.

During this long interval, a new phenomenon of Christianity
appeared. Certain scholars, in a brave effort to win the state's
full acceptance of their faith, began writing detailed explana-
tions of Christian practices and beliefs, addressed to the Emperor and other high officials. Rome had nothing to fear from
the new religion, they insisted, and Christians would prove
themselves as good and faithful citizens as any pagan subject, if
only they were allowed to worship in their own way. All things
considered, it must have seemed that the longed-for miracle
would really come to pass, that Christianity's weary night was
drawing to a close. Of course, such hopes were doomed, and
reading those earnest entreaties today, so trusting, so full of
good will and optimism, in light of the official fury that was

later to descend, is a sad and sobering experience. But for a good many years it truly seemed otherwise.

It is no cause for wonder that the church, caught up in this exciting blend of hope and desire, decided to risk putting a monument over Peter's grave—quite sensibly taking pains to disguise it—and associating with the monument a burial ground for popes. Standing on the outskirts of the vast, thousand-streeted sprawl that was Rome, tucked unobtrusively into an ordinary pagan cemetery, distant some three miles from the teeming center of the city where two million inhabitants were busy living their own lives under a benevolent ruler, the Tropaion and the complex must have seemed quite safe. At the very least, such a monument would have supplied Christians with an appropriate center, charged with high emotion, to which their hearts might turn in hopeful prayer or for solace in moments of strain and doubt.

But here the questing mind pauses, sensing something beyond. A monument and a graveyard? In reality, as is now well understood, the red wall complex took in much more than those two main structures. What, in sum, does it all suggest?

The Tropaion was not just a monument marking a grave, it was the central focus of a walled-in courtyard, the floor of which had been carefully leveled and exquisitely tiled. Judging from its dimensions, the courtyard could easily have accommodated sixty or seventy persons without crowding. Inevitably, this fact gives rise to the thought that the table-like shelf projecting from the Tropaion's middle might indeed have served as an altar for the Eucharistic sacrifice. That idea, however, was long ago rejected by the four excavators: a table standing six feet from the ground, they said, could never have been intended for an altar.

Perhaps—but that same conclusion would also have occurred in early times to any accidental intruder, and here again the theory of a hidden grave supplies the answer. The six-foot-high shelf could quite easily have been made to serve as an altar of standard height with a portable platform in place.

And what of that peculiar little window in the Tropaion's upper niche, which provided an opening through the wall to the

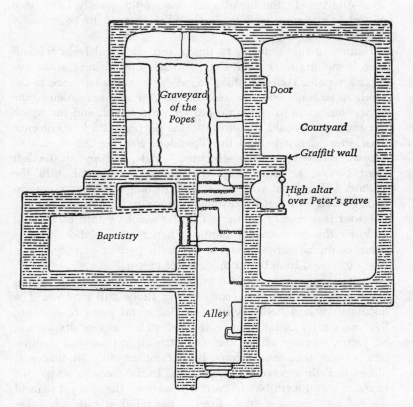

Graveyard
of the
Popes

Door

Courtyard

Graffiti wall

High altar
over Peter's grave

Baptistry

Alley

12. The red wall complex isolated from adjacent structures to show how its elements fit together as a simple church, the first such structure in the history of Christianity. Whether the area was entirely roofed over remains uncertain.

alleyway on the other side? Again, if there was any threat of an incursion while a ceremony was in progress, the materials being used—the vessels, the bread and wine—could quickly have been passed to someone waiting in the alley, thence to be speedily hidden away.

In ancient times, access to this paved alley had been shut off by a heavy ironwork door, the only such alley closure in the entire necropolis. Halfway along the alley stood the entrance to the small room built onto the rear of the Agricola mausoleum, the mysterious room in which no burials were found, and for which the excavators could discern no clear purpose. Its low entrance door, located just behind the Tropaion, was the sole means of access to the diminutive structure. Inside, occupying the left front corner, a large, deep cistern had been sunk into the ground. When filled with water, this rectangular reservoir, measuring some four feet by seven, could easily have held two people, four if necessary, immersed to the waist. Within this closed building the ceremony of baptism, in its more elaborate early form, could have been carried out with perfect privacy, effectively screened from the prying eyes of pagans.

As it happens, an authentic description of the baptismal rite commonly practiced in second-century Rome still survives. The document was actually written in Rome, no more than about five years after completion of the red wall complex. Its author, St. Justin, was one of the leaders of the city's Christian community, a man who would have been familiar with all that pertained to Peter's grave and monument. In the passage no specific locale is mentioned, but when it is read with the ground plan of the red wall complex firmly fixed in the mind, it suddenly takes on a quite stirring reality. Note that the various movements described, the going from place to place, appear to encompass a narrowly restricted area:

> We will not fail to explain how we consecrated ourselves to God when we were regenerated through Christ. Those who are convinced, and believe what we say and teach is the truth, and pledge themselves to be able to live accordingly, are

taught in prayer and fasting to ask God to forgive their past sins . . . Then we lead them to a place where there is water, and they are regenerated in the same manner in which we ourselves were regenerated. In the name of God, the Father and Lord of all, and of our Savior, Jesus Christ, and of the Holy Ghost, they then receive the washing with water . . .

There is invoked over the one who wishes to be regenerated, and who is repentant of his sins, the name of God, the Father and Lord of all, and he who leads the person to be baptized to the laver calls him by this name only . . .

After thus baptizing the one who has believed and given his assent, we escort him to the place where are assembled those whom we call brethren, to offer up sincere prayers in common for ourselves and for the baptized person, and for all other persons wherever they may be . . .

At the conclusion of the prayers we greet one another with a kiss. Then bread and a chalice containing wine mixed with water are presented to the one presiding over the brethren. He takes them and offers praise and glory to the Father of all . . . And when he who presides has celebrated the Eucharist, they whom we call deacons permit each one present to partake of the Eucharistic bread, and wine and water . . .

The picture could hardly be clearer. Standing silently in the courtyard before the Tropaion altar, the candidates for membership in the church pledge themselves to live by Christian ideals. One by one, they are then escorted through a door in the red wall, across the tiled floor of the upper graveyard, and down a short flight of steps (still in place today) into the alley, where they enter the small brick building.

At the cistern—the "laver"—they submit themselves to the "washing with water" while prayers are said and God's name invoked. The candidate is then led back through the door in the red wall to the courtyard, where his friends and family await. Here the Eucharist is celebrated, and at the conclusion of the

ceremony the new Christian for the first time is allowed to receive the consecrated bread and wine.

But if the red wall complex was used for baptism, surely it
would also have been employed for such ceremonies as the ordi-
nation of priests, the consecration of bishops, and for all the
wide variety of other special religious functions, perhaps including some marriages and even funerals. The final truth about this
ancient and hallowed spot of earth appears at last to be within
reach.

With its high altar positioned over the relics of Peter, its
walled-in area for a congregation of worshippers, its baptistry,
and its burial ground, the red wall complex in reality was the
first actual church building in Rome, in the world. More than
that, this whole deceptive clutter of brick and tile and marble
was nothing less than the first true cathedral, an anticipation in
miniature of the great guardian structure which still today soars,
exuberantly, indestructibly, above its cherished ruins.

APPENDICES

APPENDIX A

The Surviving Skeleton of St. Peter

The following table of the bones preserved in the graffiti wall is adapted from the exhaustive study performed by Dr. Venerando Correnti on all the bones found in and around Peter's grave, as published in Guarducci, *Le Reliquie di Pietro,* 96–103. Parts of the skeleton which are entirely absent are not listed herein, but they may be seen in the Correnti table. The term "fragment" is not meant to indicate size, only that the bone is less than entire.

Anatomically, it may be said that about half of Peter's skeleton remains. By volume, the figure is nearer one third.

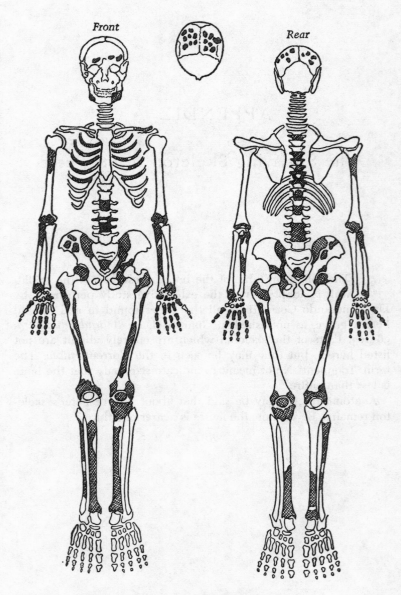

13. Surviving parts of Peter's skeleton, shown in black.

SKELETON PART   BONE REMAINING

SKULL:
top and sides (parietal)   20 fragments, left and right
forehead (frontal)   4 fragments
upper jaw (maxillary)   5 fragments
lower jaw (mandible)   2 fragments, left and right
teeth   1 canine

TRUNK:
dorsal vertebrae   12 fragments of 7 vertebrae
lumbar vertebrae   3 fragments of 2 vertebrae
ribs   16 fragments of 10 ribs

ARMS:
shoulder (clavicle)   left, 1 fragment
upper arm (humerus)   right, 2 fragments
forearm (radius)   right, 3 fragments
                                 left, 1 fragment
forearm (ulna)   left, 5 fragments

HANDS:
wrist (carpus)   left, 2 entire
                                 right, 1 fragment
palms (metacarpals)   right, 2 fragments
                                 left, 5 fragments
fingers   right, 2 fragments (1,4)
                                 left, 3 entire (1,4,5)
                                      2 fragments (2,3)

PELVIS:
girdle (ileum)   right, 6 fragments
                                 left, 5 fragments
lower (sacrum)   2 fragments

LEGS:
thigh (femur)   right, 11 fragments
                                 left, 8 fragments
knee-cap (patella)   left, entire
shin (tibia)   right, 3 fragments
                                 left, 4 fragments
shin (fibula)   right, 2 fragments

FEET: (from the ankle down, all
                                 bones are entirely absent,
                                 a peculiarity for which no
                                 explanation has been
                                 offered. But see the Notes,
                                 p. 164.)

APPENDIX B

Notes and Sources

In these Notes I have not dwelt on matters of general and church history which are already well known, but have restricted myself to items directly concerned with the main theme, citing only those primary sources on which my narrative is based. Mingled with these citations is some additional information and discussion which may hold a degree of value or interest, and which would have been out of place in the text.

The fundamental source underlying Chapters 1–6 is the Vatican's official report of the first excavations, *Esplorazioni*, etc., (see Bibliography). Rather than cite these volumes repeatedly, I mention them only for the more pertinent sections. Titles of all sources are given in short form, and may be fully identified by a glance at the bibliography.

PROLOGUE: THE ANNOUNCEMENT

Pope Paul's 1968 announcement about the bones was made in the course of one of his regular Wednesday audiences in St. Peter's Basilica (the New York *Times*, 27 June 1968, p. 1). Apparently, it was done rather suddenly, without prior notice to any of the scientists involved. The headline in the *Times* read: "Pope Says Bones Found Under Altar Are Peter's."

Five days later the same paper carried a follow-up story, a long article discussing the background of the discovery. Based on interviews with several of the scientists, it was an earnest effort, but its several distortions, errors, and oversights illustrate the difficulty many journalists faced in treating the complications of this subject (the New York *Times*, 3 July 1968, p. 2). See also *Science Digest*, December 1968, where another sincere attempt to unravel the confusion only made it worse ("St. Peter's Bones—Are They or Aren't They?"); also *Time* magazine and *Newsweek*, both for 8 July 1968, and *National Geographic*, December 1971, for some other less than successful efforts at grasping the facts.

Inevitably, in certain portions of the Christian community there was a decidedly cool reaction to Paul's announcement, in which scientific concerns were pushed aside by other interests. *The Christian Century* (10 July 1968) commented editorially: "We can't get too excited about the to-do in Rome occasioned by the Pope's announcement . . . We make no bones about the fact that we are perverse enough—or Protestant enough—to believe that no bones, not even a saint's, are sacred. If there is a connection between bone veneration and the gospel, we have yet to find it."

Even Catholic scientists were guilty on occasion of making hasty and over-casual judgments. Dr. Giovanni Judica-Cordiglia, one of Italy's leading forensic scientists, dismissed the whole matter with the remark, "The bones could be anybody's" (*Science Digest*, December 1968).

CHAPTER ONE: BURIED TOMBS

The start of the excavations and the discovery of the various sarcophagi, the Caetennius tomb and the other graves, is covered in several sections of *Esplorazioni*. Further detail was derived from Toynbee and Perkins, xv–xxii, 44–51; Kirschbaum, *Tombs*, 30–33; and from the several articles by Respighi, Josi, Ferrua, and Kaas.

Medieval accounts of the Agricola tomb, and the tomb of the gold mosaic: Kirschbaum, *Tombs,* 35–36; Toynbee and Perkins, 30–32.

Several accounts of the Ostoria Chelidon sarcophagus state that the body was found embalmed and intact, clothed in purple garments, etc. (for instance, Toynbee and Perkins, 106, and Guarducci, *Tomb,* 68). But this is an error specifically corrected by one of those present at the opening of the sarcophagus: "The body was not embalmed. Only the bones are preserved" (Kirschbaum, *Tombs,* 217). The error may have arisen, strangely enough, from Josi, 4.

"Mix the wine, drink deep . . ." Toynbee and Perkins, 58, where the whole inscription is given in English.

The history of the Vatican area since Constantine, and of the two basilicas, may be had in a number of works. I have used the more recent volumes of Lees-Milne and Hollis; also Toynbee and Perkins, 195–239, and Guarducci, *Tomb,* 44–59.

Primary sources for the excavations beneath the body of the basilica are not voluminous as to detail, and most are available only in Italian. The official report, concentrating its attention on Peter's grave and shrine and the immediately surrounding area, leaves much information about the other tombs unrecorded. Early articles by Josi, Ferrua, etc., filled this gap to some extent, but the discrepancy was at last comprehensively supplied by Jocelyn Toynbee and John Ward Perkins in their scholarly work, *The Shrine of St. Peter and the Vatican Excavations,* 1957.

CHAPTER TWO: STREET OF THE DEAD

Tombs flanking the Caetennius mausoleum: Toynbee and Perkins, 24–117, *passim* (the descriptions do not proceed in sequence but are grouped according to artistic and architectural categories). Also, Kirschbaum, *Tombs,* 27–45, and the articles by Josi, Ferrua (1941, 1942, 1952), and Belvederi.

The Valerius tomb: The cloaked figure in the central niche of this tomb is interpreted by some as representing not a member of the Valerius family, but the god Apollo Harpocrates. I have preferred the opinion expressed in Toynbee and Perkins, 85. For the sketched heads of Jesus and Peter, and the inscription in the central niche, see Guarducci, *Tombs,* 144–47, Kirschbaum, *Tombs,* 28–29, Toynbee and Perkins, 14–17, and O'Connor, 179–82.

"We let the workmen . . ." Kirschbaum, *Tombs,* 34. For further detail on the interior of this tomb, see Toynbee and Perkins, 72–74.

A summary listing of all the burials found in the tombs under the basilica, including names and family relationships, and in some cases occupations, is given in Toynbee and Perkins, Appendix A.

Details of the terrain on which the Roman necropolis stood and the difficulties that faced Constantine's engineers: Kirschbaum, *Tombs,* 42–44, Toynbee and Perkins, 197–98.

Pope Sylvester's part in the building of the first basilica is recorded in *Liber Pontificalis,* where it is expressly stated that the first suggestion for erecting a basilica over Peter's grave came from this pope. Whether this means that the whole concept was Sylvester's from the start, or that he may have responded to an offer from Constantine, is not clear. In the same section of the *Liber Pontificalis* occurs the reference to the bronze coffin.

Nero's Circus: A principal concern of the excavators in the early phases of the work was with finding some trace of the circus or arena of Nero, whose ruins supposedly underlay the south side of the basilica. This hope was connected with claims in early documents that Peter's grave lay adjacent to the arena. No sign of the circus was found, however, and the plausible explanation was offered that the structure could have been built of perishable materials, perhaps mostly wood and earthen banks, rather than of stone and marble. Later, however, the excavators came upon an inscription over the entrance to a tomb which made it certain that Nero's circus had indeed once stood in the vicinity. The inscription, engraved on marble, mentions a clause from the will of the tomb's owner, Popilius Heracla, directing that his mausoleum be situated "on the Vatican near the Circus." If the dead man's wishes in this respect had not been honored, the inscription would scarcely have bothered alluding to the clause. (See Kirschbaum, *Tombs*, 21–22; Josi, 6; Respighi, 5.)

CHAPTER THREE: BENEATH THE HIGH ALTAR

All the early documentary references to Peter are handily collected or mentioned in O'Connor, *Peter in Rome*, where they are discussed and evaluated (many of O'Connor's conclusions, as to the individual worth or import of these documents, are open to serious disagreement, an exercise not pertinent here). For further extended treatment of certain of the early documents see Guarducci, *Tombs*, 25–43, Toynbee and Perkins, 127–33, Respighi (1942).

"When you were young . . ." John 21:18

"So put away all malice . . ." 1 Peter 2:1–3

"Their death was turned . . ." Howe and Harrer, *Roman Literature*, 633.

"Marcellus, not asking . . ." M. R. James, 336.

The "memorial shrine" supposedly erected in the first century by Pope Anacletus is discussed in Kirschbaum, *Tombs*, 132–33; the original record is in *Liber Pontificalis*. For a highly probable confusion with the later Pope Anicetus, see the text above, p. 67.

The reference by the priest Gaius to the "Tropaion" is preserved only in Eusebius, *History of the Church*. Gaius' remark was called forth during a controversy with the Montanists, in which the graves of certain apostles were appealed to as conferring apostolic sanction on various teachings. See Kirschbaum, *Tombs*, 78–79, O'Connor, 85–101.

The belief of Monsignor Kaas that Peter's body would be found in a bronze sarcophagus is in Guarducci, *Reliquie-messa*, 82–83; also a letter from Dr. Guarducci to the author. Kaas' settled conviction in this regard, as Dr. Guarducci believes, certainly must have played a part in his unfortunate blunder at the graffiti wall by blinding him to all other possibilities: see Chapter 6 and its Notes, 160. On this same topic, see Kirschbaum, *Tombs*, 51–52.

"The man who desires to pray . . ." Gregory of Tours, quoting a description supplied by his deacon, Agiulph, after a visit to the basilica, in *De Gloria Martyrum*, quoted here from Kirschbaum, *Tombs*, 157.

"Unspeakable iniquities . . ." Quoted from Toynbee and Perkins, 228.

The accident of 1594 at the shrine: Kirschbaum, *Tombs*, 61, 220, and Lees-Milne, 225.

The inspection made by Hartmann Grisar at the Niche of the Pallia: Grisar, *Le Tombe*, 19–23; see also *Analecta Romana*, 1899.

The original basilica shrine: Eventually the excavators were able to reconstruct, in some detail, the original Constantinian shrine over Peter's grave. Essential to the success of this effort was a fifth-century reliquary known as the Samagher Casket, then stored in the Lateran Museum in Rome. The four sides of this box have liturgical scenes carved into them, one of which, it was at length realized, depicts Peter's shrine in its original appearance. The complete facts about this unique artifact have been gathered by Dr. Guarducci into a pamphlet, *La Capsella Eburnea di Samagher*, 1978.

CHAPTER FOUR: PETER'S GRAVE

The principal primary source for reconstructing the actual sequence of the excavations under the high altar is found in Kirschbaum, *Tombs*, 53–94. None of the other participants provided any record with like detail. But Kirschbaum's account, unfortunately rather bare and somewhat confusing, must be interpreted in the light of several other sources, particularly Respighi, "Esplorazioni recenti"; Ferrua, "Il sepolcro"; Josi, "Gli scavi"; Toynbee and Perkins, 137–66; and Belvederi, "La tomba."

"Expectantly, we turned . . ." Kirschbaum, *Tombs*, 66.

Discovery of the graffiti wall: Esplorazioni, 129–30, Kirschbaum, *Tombs*, 67.

"merged into the darkness . . ." Kirschbaum, *Tombs*, 77.

The initial discovery of the empty marble repository in the

graffiti wall is covered at some length in Kirschbaum, *Tombs*, 71–73. See also *Esplorazioni*, 162, and Guarducci, *Le Reliquie*, 19–21.

The entry into the central chamber, Peter's grave, is given by Kirschbaum himself in *Tombs*, 74–78 (see also 91, 195–96), and *Esplorazioni*, 195–96. A rather reticent man when writing of his own part in the excavations, Kirschbaum neglected to describe his actual finding of the bones under the red wall, though he fully discusses the bones themselves, specifying their location and condition when uncovered. My picture of the moment is based on a study of all available contemporary sources, primary and secondary. While I cannot guarantee that the finding of the bones occurred during this first entry, rather than at some subsequent entry, the tendency of the evidence makes it very probable.

That Pius XII was immediately informed of the discovery of the red wall bones, and was present at their unearthing, is mentioned only in the New York *Times*, 22 August 1949. It is hardly a point, in any case, which needs documentary support.

A circumstantial description of the various bones at the moment they were taken from under the red wall is not supplied by Kirschbaum, nor by any of the other participants. My description is based on the later detailed analysis of them by Dr. Correnti, printed in *Le Reliquie*, 107–23.

For the early medical verdict on the red wall bones see Kirschbaum, *Tombs*, 195–96, Guarducci, *Le Reliquie*, 15–16, and O'Connor, 196.

CHAPTER FIVE: THE RED WALL COMPLEX

The coins: A complete listing, with illustrations, of all the coins found in and around Peter's grave and shrine is supplied in *Esplorazioni*, 225–44.

For the excavators' interpretation of the various structures comprising the red wall complex see the articles of Josi, Respighi, Ferrua; also, Kirschbaum, *Tombs*, 79–83, Toynbee and

Perkins, 144–51. For a later commentary on the earlier conclusions, offering a few refinements, see Prandi, *La Zona, passim.*

The open courtyard before the Tropaion: It is not explained in the several reports just why the excavators should have decided that this supposedly open area, surrounded by walls, might not have been covered by some sort of roof. Since only a relatively short portion of one wall remains (the red wall), and nothing can be judged as to its top, it would seem possible that the courtyard had in fact originally been roofed over. Certainly it is reasonable to think that protection would have been given to the Tropaion itself, as well as the grave's closure slab under it. That probability, moreover, is supported by the rather fresh, unweathered appearance the red plaster presented when first uncovered. The same, in general, might be said for the upper burial ground, which now is also thought to have been open to the skies.

"dwindled to a few centimeters . . ." Kirschbaum, *Tombs,* 85.

Dating of the red wall complex: Kirschbaum, *Tombs,* 80, Toynbee and Perkins, 262–65. The mid-second-century date assigned to the complex by the excavators was subsequently confirmed by the excavations of Adriano Prandi (1956–57), as reported in his book, *La Zona Archeologica,* 3–37, 92–93.

The work of Prandi negated one of the excavators' pet theories, that concerning the burials surrounding Peter's grave. Originally, eleven such burials were uncovered, matching the claim in old documents that exactly eleven early popes lay in the close vicinity of Peter's body. Prandi's operation, however, turned up some thirty burials, whole or in remnants. With that, the claim regarding the eleven popes was forgotten—though why the eleven might not be counted among the thirty is still unclear.

The angled grave under the Tropaion: Kirschbaum, *Tombs,* 78, 91. The excavators rightly stress the peculiar angling of the central chamber and the closure slab, in relation to the red wall, as proving that the empty space below the monument was once an actual, full-length grave. No other interpretation supplies a reasonable cause for this subtle but striking anomaly.

The word "Tropaion"—and its possible meanings—has been exhaustively studied, especially by Christine Mohrmann (see Bibliography). Almost all scholars now agree that the word can only mean a monument built over a grave containing a body. Some critics had insisted that the word might indicate nothing more than a commemorative monument set up at any random location, or that it simply marked the site of Peter's execution. The linguistic studies, together with the incontrovertible fact of the angled chamber, have laid such objections to rest. See Kirschbaum, *Tombs*, 110–14, Toynbee and Perkins, 154–57, O'Connor, 95–101.

CHAPTER SIX: STROKE OF FATE

"Has the tomb of St. Peter . . ." Radio broadcast of Pius XII, Christmas 1950, reported in the New York *Times*, 24 December.

"some human bones . . ." *Esplorazioni*, 165.

The *Petros Eni* graffito found by Ferrua in the repository of the graffiti wall was first reported by him in *Il Messaggero*, 16 June 1952. A strange situation later developed, which saw Ferrua treating the bit of masonry almost as his personal property, in effect withholding it from study by other experts. He included an incorrect sketch of it in an article written for *La Civiltà Cattolica*, and later (1954) discussed it at an archaeological congress in Aix-en-Provence. But not until 1957 did he relinquish the artifact itself for permanent storage in the Vatican. Its surrender at that time was at least partly due to pressures brought by Dr. Guarducci, who was curious to see the inscription in the original. As it turned out, her instincts were sound. See Kirschbaum, *Tombs*, 221, Guarducci, *Retrouvé*, 60, and the Notes below, 166.

Monsignor Kaas and the marble repository: The truth regarding this episode went unrecognized for more than twenty years, until Dr. Guarducci and her colleagues were able to reconstruct the actual sequence of events. See Guarducci, *Le Reliquie,*

37–40, and her *Reliquie-messa,* 13–14, 82–92. Also see Chapter 8, and the Notes below, 167.

CHAPTER SEVEN: THE WOODEN BOX

Dr. Guarducci's own extensive writings remain the principal source for reconstructing the detailed sequence of her pivotal role in the finding of Peter's relics. Basic, as an overview, is her *St. Pierre Retrouvé,* 1974 (only this French translation from the Italian is now available), but this must be supplemented by her earlier writings, particularly *I Graffiti* (1958), and *Le Reliquie* (1965), with its important follow-up pamphlet of 1967.

In addition, I have had the pleasure of direct discussions with Dr. Guarducci through correspondence and in person. Now nearing eighty, she continues with her work, an inspiration in her field, her energies unabated after almost sixty years of steady accomplishment. The total of her contributions to scholarly journals, on a wide range of archaeological and epigraphical subjects, both Roman and Greek, has continued to mount and now exceeds a remarkable three hundred. A bibliography of her writings up to 1976 has been issued by the *Accademia Nazionale dei Lincei,* Rome. The cornerstone of her career continues to be the two now-standard collections: *Inscriptiones Creticae,* four volumes, Rome, 1935–50, and *Epigrafia Greca,* four volumes, Rome, 1967–77.

Decipherment of the Valerius inscription: See four works by Guarducci; *Cristo e San Pietro,* etc., which contains a full report on the work, *I Graffiti,* II, 397–403, *Tomb,* 144–46, and *Retrouvé,* 62–64.

Dr. Guarducci's amazed reaction to her first sight of the graffiti wall is in a letter to the author; also, *Retrouvé,* 65–66.

Finding of the wooden box: Le Reliquie, 20–21, and *Reliquie-messa,* 5–6. The conversation between Giovanni Segoni and Dr. Guarducci is in *Retrouvé,* 105–6.

The separate bones found in the wooden box in September 1953 are not enumerated or described by Dr. Guarducci. My description of them is based on the analysis later supplied by Dr. Correnti in *Le Reliquie*, 134–44.

Dr. Guarducci's crucial decision, prompted solely by scientific habit, to set aside the graffiti wall bones for further routine study is in *Retrouvé*, 108. In the same place she notes the date on which the bones were locked away: 25 September 1953. Thus, for ten years these bones, later to be identified as Peter's, lay unregarded in the Vatican. It is this "lost" period, especially, that many journalists in their professional hurry found it difficult to account for, or to view without suspicion.

CHAPTER EIGHT: WHAT THE GRAFFITI HID

Dr. Guarducci's pioneering effort at the graffiti wall was reported by her in massive detail in the three large volumes of *I Graffiti*. The third of these volumes contains a complete series of close-up photographs of the wall's whole surface, showing with admirable clarity the entire network of names and coded inscriptions (that is, the individual scratches in the tangled mass may be clearly followed). Admittedly, for the unpracticed eye it requires some patient study to recognize all the forms and shapes identified by Dr. Guarducci—and perhaps her interpretations here and there might, as some insist, be questioned. But that is hardly surprising when dealing with so arcane a code piled up in such a welter.

Further discussion of the mystical cryptography theory was presented by Dr. Guarducci in her articles "Il Fenomino orientale," 1964, and "Dal Gioco letterale," 1978.

"He said that with his own . . ." Eusebius, *Life of Constantine,* quoted from Guarducci, *Tomb,* 123.

The Peter symbol: Guarducci, *I Graffiti,* I, 385–478, which provides a comprehensive discussion of the symbol itself, its varied uses, development, background, etc. See also her volumes *Tomb,* 107–12, and *Retrouvé,* 72–73.

"He was known throughout . . ." Eusebius, *Theophania,* IV, 7, quoted from Guarducci, *Tomb,* 9. Of course, this proof of a widespread clinging to the memory of Peter during the centuries after his death did not come as any great surprise to those familiar with the Christian art of the catacombs. Second in importance only to Christ as a subject of catacombal art, Peter is represented on the moldering walls of these eerie passageways beneath the environs of Rome more than three hundred times. The number of different scenes and incidents depicted from his life, all found in the Gospels, is nearly thirty (Hertling and Kirschbaum, *Catacombs,* 242–44).

CHAPTER NINE: THE BONES EXAMINED

Dr. Correnti's study of the red wall bones was fully reported by him in *Le Reliquie,* 93–124. He gives a lengthy table listing every bone and fragment, along with a complete set of illustrations. See also Guarducci, *Retrouvé,* 109–10.

"A recess under the . . ." Kirschbaum, in Hollis, *The Papacy,* 17. An earlier statement by Kirschbaum to similar effect occurs in his own book, *Tombs,* first published in German in 1957. It clearly demonstrates the anguished indecision produced in the Vatican by the red wall bones:

A small heap of bones was discovered beneath the lowest niche of the red wall. They were therefore in the area of the ancient central grave, which we have identified as that of the apostle . . . It might be surmised that scattered remains had at one time been collected and placed beneath the red wall. In that case, an anatomical investigation would have showed that they belonged to different skeletons. Medical examination, however, gave the contrary verdict, i.e., that all these bones belonged to one and the same person. That person was further described as an elderly and vigorous man. The skull is missing . . .

All we can say is that the bones were removed from a grave now recognized to have been that of St. Peter, and that they were in fact the bones of an elderly man. At the time of his death Peter was elderly. Great responsibility, to be sure, is incurred in the attribution of any bones to St. Peter. But there would be just as much responsibility at stake in ignoring earthly remains of the chief apostle, if they had in fact been found. As things now are, it is probably impossible to pass a final judgment. Yet we have to emphasize the fact—which must be seriously considered—that the bones of an elderly man were discovered within the precincts of the apostle's grave, and that a thousand or more years ago they were acknowledged to be such . . . Can we seriously imagine that at some indefinite period some indeterminate bones were placed precisely at this spot, which as we have seen was the focus of a constantly increasing devotion, and that, in consequence, we have been seriously misled? The question we prefer to leave open . . . (195–96).

The real source of the difficulty, of course, was the hurried and mistaken verdict rendered on the red wall bones by Dr. Galeazzi-Lisi and other medical men. No report of this early examination was ever published, officially or otherwise, so there is little that may be said of it. However, it appears certain that these doctors took their task rather too casually, not recognizing that the study properly required a professional anatomist. The speed with which the first verdict was rendered contrasts sharply with the time taken up by Correnti's later definitive study.

The absence of foot bones: There has been little or no comment on this peculiarity of the graffiti wall cache—peculiar because of the *total* absence of the bones below both ankles. That these pieces might have been lost because of their small size is no answer, since many bones from the fingers of a similar size *are* present, showing how much care was used with these relics. One possible explanation, admittedly beyond proof, does leap to mind: Might there not be some link between the missing foot bones, and the tradition that Peter was crucified head downward? With his feet nailed to the upper part of the cross, whether separately or together, Roman executioners in removing the body certainly would not have hesitated to sever the feet, should the extraction of the heavy nail or nails from the wood have proved at all difficult.

Dr. Correnti's examination of the graffiti wall bones was fully reported by him in *Le Reliquie*, 134–57. Again, he supplies a complete table, as well as illustrations. He also gives precise anthropological values for certain of the more important pieces in support of his decision as to the individual's sex (141–44).

CHAPTER TEN: THE PETER THEORY

The conversation between Drs. Correnti and Guarducci, and its consequence in turning her thoughts toward the true identity of the graffiti wall bones, is in Guarducci, *Retrouvé*, 112–14. See also *Le Reliquie*, 19–24, and *Reliquie-messa*, 6.

In her first conception of the Peter theory, Dr. Guarducci may have been aided to an extent by some prior speculations of the four original excavators. In the years after the first discovery of the cavity in the graffiti wall, Josi, Ferrua, and Kirschbaum had continued to be curious about its function. In their writings each had suggested that the hidden space might, in some undetermined way, actually have been connected with Peter's remains. Each considered whether it might have been used as a temporary depository in earlier periods, either for all the bones or for the skull alone (see, for example, Kirschbaum, *Tombs*, 196–200). These ideas were linked to theorizing about another archaeological site in Rome—now covered by the ancient Church of San Sebastiano—where mysterious devotions to both Peter and Paul had flourished for some decades before the advent of Constantine. But such speculations, highly tentative as the excavators admitted, perhaps did no more for Dr. Guarducci than prepare her mind for the sudden onset of her own hypothesis. The real trigger, appropriately, was provided by an inscription, the *Petros Eni* graffito. (The literature on the San Sebastiano site is large; for an introduction see O'Connor, 135–58, also Toynbee and Perkins, 167–82.)

Dr. Guarducci's study of the *Petros Eni* graffito is given in

I Graffiti, II, 396–402. See also her description in *Tomb,* 131–33, and *Le Reliquie,* 37–40.

In this same connection, Dr. Guarducci asserts that the upper of the two lines on the plaster (the ΠΕΤΡ . . .) shows a decided convex curvature from left to right, as if the unknown writer had used his elbow for a pivot. She sees the conjectured right termination of this upper line as being too far lowered to permit the second line (the ΕΝΙ) to have originally been longer, since it would then have run across the end of the drooping upper line. Considerable discussion has centered on this claim, and several scholars have registered strong disagreement. The materials themselves are too fragile and tenuous to permit an absolute decision, but it must be said that Dr. Guarducci's theory does indeed appear quite possible. See *I Graffiti,* II, 396–407, *Tomb,* 131–33, and *Reliquie-messa,* 53–65.

The first audience of Dr. Guarducci with Paul VI, and their later meetings, are recorded in Guarducci, *Retrouvé,* 115–17. See also Menen, *Rock,* 57–65.

Examination of the animal bones, the cloth, and the soil: Le Reliquie, 161–82. See also Guarducci, *Retrouvé,* 118–22. Examination of the contents of the Lateran reliquary is reported in *Reliquie-messa,* 80–82.

No official report has yet appeared on the Lateran skull. In its absence, perhaps several suggestions might be made. The paucity of bones available for study obviously would have negated any effort to determine such fundamentals as age, sex, and body type. And yet Dr. Correnti was unequivocal in his opinion that no conflict existed between the Lateran skull and the graffiti wall bones, among which were some skull fragments. Logically, there appear to be only three methods by which this certainty could have been reached:

1) The Lateran bones were submitted to radiocarbon dating and their absolute age was found to be a good deal less than the requisite nineteen hundred years. Dr. Guarducci hints at this outcome when she invites her readers to "reflect" on the fact that the first traceable record of the Lateran skull dates to only the eleventh century.

2) All fragments from the two groups were compared and no exact duplication was uncovered. This would leave intact the claims of both sets of bones to authenticity.

3) One or more of the Lateran cranial fragments showed traces of the suture, and the degree of ossification showed the individual's age at death as less than fifty years. Of course, it is not wholly impossible that the Correnti study turned up information of quite a different order.

The discovery by Dr. Guarducci that none of the original four excavators had any knowledge of Monsignor Kaas' action in removing the graffiti wall bones and quietly storing them away is in *Reliquie-messa*, 12–14. See also Guarducci, *Retrouvé*, 124–26.

After the Pope's 1968 announcement about the bones, the four excavators were sought by reporters for interviews, but apparently only Josi was available. To the newsmen he insisted that he had taken no part whatever in the work of Dr. Guarducci, had "nothing to say" about the Pope's sudden announcement, and in fact was completely "out of the picture" (the New York *Times*, 27 June 1968). This response, naturally, left the reporters even more puzzled than before, since so far as they were aware Josi had been a key mover in the excavations. But nothing more was said.

Even today it is not easy to understand why these four men should have been left out of the latter phases of the work, beginning with Correnti's study of the graffiti wall bones in the fall of 1962. And a large portion of their obvious resentment, undoubtedly, arose from thoughts of what might have happened had they been told of the existence of the bones at any time during the ten years (1953–62) in which they lay ignored in a cupboard at the Vatican. The marble cavity in the graffiti wall, found empty so far as they knew, had already captured their attention to the point of theorizing about its possible links to Peter's remains (see above, p. 165). This view deserves some sympathy, since it is true that if Dr. Guarducci had informed these men about her accidental discovery of the bones, at the time it occurred in the fall of 1953, the denouement of 1968 might have taken place more than a decade earlier. In that case, much of the confusion and indecision over the red wall bones would have been avoided, and the troublesome interlude during which the graffiti wall bones lay "forgotten," would never have occurred. Detectable in all of this, it must be said, is a certain antagonism, on both sides, which prevented mention of the graffiti wall bones even in a casual or offhand way. Signs of such a personal strain between the parties are not wanting in the literature.

Kirschbaum's acceptance of the Peter theory was expressed to Dr. Guarducci in a letter of December 1964, mentioned in *Reliquie-messa,* 13. See also Kirschbaum's article in *Archivum Historiae Pontificiae,* where he points out the fact that he and several others before Dr. Guarducci had suggested a possible connection between the marble repository and Peter's remains. Quite correctly, he says that it would not have been amiss had Dr. Guarducci seen fit in her writings to make some mention of these earlier speculations.

For a full presentation of Dr. Guarducci's evidence in favor of the bones, see her *Le Reliquie,* 72–77, *Retrouvé,* 117–44, and *Reliquie-messa,* 6–8.

The five scientists who reviewed Dr. Guarducci's proofs are listed in *Reliquie-messa,* 8–9. They were, from the University of Rome, Professor Giovanni Beccati and Professor Guglielmo de Angelis d'Ossat; from the University of Bari, Professor Virgilio Paladini; from the University of Perugia, Professor Filippo Magi; and Professor Gianfilippo Carettoni, Director of excavations at the Roman Forum. It seems not to have been the function of these men to judge general conclusions about the identity of the bones, but only to pass on the soundness of the scientific elements involved in the theory, along with permissible interpretation of that evidence.

Testimony of Giovanni Segoni: The notarized affidavit of foreman Segoni, dated 7 January 1965 and now in the Vatican archives, makes the following main points. When he inspected the cavity sometime in 1941 it contained a "certain quantity of bones," all stark white. At the order of Monsignor Kaas, and in his presence, he removed the bones, placed them in a wooden box, and personally stored the box with others in the small room behind the chapel of St. Columban. In September 1953 he recovered this same box for Dr. Guarducci. A second workman, it later developed, had also been occupied nearby at the moment when Segoni removed the bones, and recalled the circumstances (*Reliquie-messa*, 11–12; *Retrouvé*, 128).

CHAPTER ELEVEN: DECISION

For the several leading objections to Dr. Guarducci's 1965 book and theory, and her replies thereto, see her 1967 pamphlet, *Reliquie-messa*, 24–53, *passim*. See also her article "Infundate" and her book *Retrouvé*, 124–26. For coverage of the more extended objections see the articles in the bibliography below for Carcopino, Coppo, Ruysschaert (1965), Smothers (1965), and Toynbee (1965); also O'Connor, *Peter*, 170–205, *passim*.

Color-testing of the cloth: *Reliquie-messa*, 65–74.

Inspection of the repository: *Reliquie-messa*, 14–17.

The Constantius coin: *Reliquie-messa*, 74–75.

(For the three items above see also *Retrouvé*, 119–33.)

Dr. Correnti's discussion of the Carbon-14 test is fully presented in *Reliquie-messa*, 77–78. It might be noted that today, more than ten years after Correnti's opinion was first expressed, radiocarbon dating technique has undergone considerable refinement. Much less material is now required, perhaps as little as the size of a fingernail, and the plus-or-minus factor has also been drastically reduced, some authorities claiming an accuracy of perhaps two percent, which would put it under fifty years. Despite all reasons offered to the contrary, there can be no doubt that the test should someday be made.

Chemical tests were also performed on the bits of red plaster and the marble chips found in the wooden box. These were proved to match the red wall and the slabs lining the repository. See *Reliquie-messa*, 9–11, and *Retrouvé*, 117.

An eyewitness description of the ceremonies attending return of the bones to the graffiti wall is in Guarducci, *Retrouvé,* 147–48. See also the New York *Times,* 28 June 1968.

CHAPTER TWELVE: THE ANCIENT SILENCE

For Roman law respecting the burial of criminals, see O'Connor, *Peter,* 93–94, 128; also *Dictionary of Roman Law,* American Philosophical Society, 1953.

Recovery of Peter's body: The manner in which Peter's body was, or might have been, recovered after his crucifixion at one time threatened to become a minor controversy on its own. Some respected scholars insisted that the body could not have been saved, that it *must* have disappeared, since after death on the cross it would have been burned—perhaps lost in a heap of martyrs' corpses—and any remaining bones would have been scattered. At best, this was an argument in a vacuum, there being nothing whatever known of the true circumstances, not even whether Peter died by himself or with others. That the recovery *could* have been managed either through bribery of some minor official, or else surreptitiously, must be admitted by all. And at least two instances of a martyr's body being stolen out of the hands of the Romans—one definite, the other highly probable— can be documented (the fact that the incidents took place some hundred years after Peter's death does not, in my view, lessen their relevance. The usual charge that the "cult of the martyrs" did not arise until long afterward has no bearing on the special case of Peter).

About the year 165, St. Justin and six Christian companions were executed in Rome. A contemporary account tells what happened next: "The holy martyrs went out, glorifying God, to the customary place, and were beheaded, and fulfilled their testimony by the confession of their Savior. And some of the faithful took their bodies by stealth and laid them in a convenient place, the grace of our Lord Jesus Christ working with them . . ." (*Martyrdom of St. Justin,* quoted from Fremantle, 196). It might be noted that the unnamed "convenient place" in which the bodies were interred, at least temporarily, may well have been the upper burial ground adjacent to the Tropaion. The site had been completed only a few years before, and could easily have accommodated seven bodies.

About a decade before the death of Justin and his friends, there occurred the martyrdom of St. Polycarp, in Smyrna, and the preservation of his bones very probably affords another instance of recovery by stealth. After Polycarp's death under the sword, his body was burned by the Romans, precisely to prevent its being taken for veneration by the faithful. But, as the old record relates, the faithful were not deterred: "We took up his bones, being of more value than precious stones and more excellent than gold, and laid them apart in a suitable place" (Barry, 74). The writer does not specify that the saint's charred bones were actually stolen from Roman custody, but under the circumstances that conclusion may be taken as certain—neither the writer nor his readers needed to have such matters explained. The use of the phrases "a convenient place" and "a suitable place" in the accounts of Justin and Polycarp also strongly indicates that the locations of such graves were customarily kept secret.

A third example of the attempts to recover the mutilated bodies or charred remains of martyred Christians, this time by both stealth and bribery, occurred in the year 177 at Lyons, though in this case the effort failed. After a sudden, ferocious, but short-lived local persecution (fired by dark rumors of "Thyestean banquets and Oedipean unions") the heaped remains of perhaps a dozen martyrs were committed to a guard of Roman soldiers. The contemporary account explains:

> Those that were suffocated in the prison they threw to the dogs, watching carefully by night and day lest we should give any of them burial. After that they exposed what the beasts and the fire had left, part torn, part charred, and the heads of the rest with the trunks; these likewise they left unburied, and watched them for many days with a guard of soldiers . . . There was great sorrow because we could not bestow the bodies in the earth. For night did not help us towards this, nor

money persuade, nor prayers shame, but they watched every way, as though they would derive some great profit from the martyr's loss of burial . . . So the bodies of the martyrs, after being subjected to all kinds of contumely and exposed for six days, were then burnt and reduced to ashes by the impious, and swept into the river Rhône which flows hard by, that not a fragment of them might be left on earth. (*Letter from Lyons and Vienne,* quoted from Fremantle, 208–9)

"Secretly, it is true . . ." The Emperor Julian in his treatise *Against the Galileans,* quoted from Fremantle, 261. Certain scholars have not know quite what to make of this remark of Julian's about Peter's grave and have ended by passing it off, rather abruptly, as worthless. "A tradition such as this, appearing for the first time in the fourth century, is surely unfounded," wrote D. W. O'Connor (*Peter in Rome,* 103). But this is much too hasty a judgment, obviously the result of a momentary lapse in critical balance. Elsewhere in his book, for instance, O'Connor willingly accepts the testimony of Porphyry against Peter's having founded the Roman church, even though Porphyry's opinion dates to two centuries after Peter's death, and is available only in the work of another writer (*Peter in Rome,* 88). Here is the passage from *Against the Galileans* in which Julian's remark occurs:

At any rate, neither Paul nor Matthew nor Luke nor Mark ventured to call Jesus God. But the worthy John, since he perceived that a great number of the people in many of the towns of Greece and Italy had already been infected by this disease, and because he heard, I suppose, that even the tombs of Peter and Paul were being worshipped—secretly, it is true, but still he did hear this—he, I say, was the first to venture to call Jesus God . . .

Julian's easy reference to the graves of Peter and Paul as already being venerated at the time when John wrote his Gospel (A.D. 90–100) is clearly an offhand mention of a fact that Julian takes to have been long and widely accepted. His obvious source would have been his own uncle, Constantine, who must certainly have learned about the tradition of a secret grave from Pope Sylvester when plans for the first basilica were being formed. Thus the tradition did not "appear" for the first time in the fourth century, but was then publicly acknowledged, at the same time, be it noted, that the location of the hidden grave itself was revealed.

Design of the Tropaion: It may perhaps be asserted that the monument's neutral design was merely a result of the prevalent tendency among early Christians to adopt whatever was good and serviceable in Roman culture. That may be true to an extent, but the point to be stressed is the *total* absence in the design of any feature which could link the structure to Christianity—a simple cross, for instance, or the usual symbol of a fish, or even some rendition of the key-like Peter symbol, to mention the obvious.

The graffiti wall: If this wall was erected during the early part of the decade 250–60, then transfer of the bones from the grave to the marble repository would have been the work of Pope Cornelius (251–53). Interestingly, the *Liber Pontificalis* credits him with a "translation" of Peter's remains (and Paul's), though the reference is obscure and has no obvious relation to the graffiti wall. If the wall was built toward the latter part of the decade, during the fierce persecution of Valerian (257–60), then Pope Sixtus II would have been responsible for transfer of the bones. The *Liber Pontificalis*, however, has no reference that can be so interpreted. Sixtus himself died a martyr when he was beheaded in the catacombs by Roman soldiers. He was at the time engaged in celebrating mass for the martyrs buried there, an act which infringed Valerian's law closing Christian cemeteries. Between Cornelius and Sixtus, two other popes had brief reigns, Lucius and Stephen. While either of these could have been responsible for the transfer, no document links their names with the Tropaion or with Peter's remains.

The conspiracy of silence: Of course the whole Christian movement during the early years involved a fundamental secrecy regarding membership, and this pervasive atmosphere would have made it natural and easy to extend the silence to Peter's remains. After all, had not Jesus declared to the apostle, "Thou art Peter, and upon this rock I will build my church"? In light of these forthright words, it is not surprising that, in addition to Peter's living presence, Christians should have come to regard his physical body as in some sense partaking of the Rock on which the church was built, and would desire to preserve it, at all costs, for as far into the future as possible. And it is hardly outside the experience of human nature that this attitude was at last given full physical expression when the red wall complex— the first real church building—was constructed over and around Peter's body.

It might be observed that a theory of deliberate silence, applied to the living Peter, would also explain the almost total dearth of reliable information concerning the last two decades or so of his life. After his miraculous delivery from prison, it must be remembered, he carried the brand of an escaped convict— and King Herod was so angered at losing this particular prisoner that he had the unfortunate jailers executed (Acts 12:19). Looked at in this light, it is perhaps understandable why Peter's whereabouts thereafter, and his movements, should have been left almost completely unrecorded in contemporary documents, and especially that explicit mention of him is oddly absent from certain letters of Paul.

Diocletian's persecution began in the year 303, while Marcellinus was pope. Little is known of him and no document offers any clue as to whether it was at his command that the bones were transferred from grave to wall. A confusion in the records makes it uncertain whether Marcellinus reigned until the year 309, or whether another man, named Marcellus, served briefly 308–9, with the office vacant during 304–8, when the persecution reached its bloody height.

Constantine and Sylvester: The relations between Emperor and Pope, personal and official, would certainly have played a part in Sylvester's decision about keeping or revealing the secret location of Peter's bones. And the history of their association, as much of it as is known, shows that there was never a time when the Pope could have placed full and irrevocable confidence in the Emperor's Christian orthodoxy. During the twenty years or so in which they reigned together, there was continual embroilment over church affairs, organizational matters, the deliberations of church councils, implicit questions as to the Pope's primacy, and the need to deal with heresy, particularly Arianism, which at one period Constantine himself viewed sympathetically. And perhaps—just perhaps—Sylvester may very early have decided that the secret of the bones need *never* be revealed. He knew with absolute certainty that Peter's bones lay within the sumptuous marble shrine then standing over the grave. That the bones were in the graffiti wall, rather than in the central chamber, may not have struck Sylvester and his companions with the same force felt today. And it is in this area that Dr. Guarducci's reasoning on the point has some relevance. The factors she cites as explaining the *removal* of the bones from grave to repository make much more sense when used to explain why the bones were permitted to *remain* in the repository.

Julian the Apostate: Some modern scholars tend to absolve the Emperor Julian from being an actual persecutor of Christians, mostly, it seems, because he did not order any wholesale bloodletting, as had some of his predecessors. But the whole tendency of his brief reign was undoubtedly in that direction, and if he had lived, the history of Rome and of Christianity in the latter part of the fourth century, and for who knows how long thereafter, would have been vastly different. All this is clearly set forth by Giuseppe Ricciotti in his definitive scholarly work, *Julian the Apostate,* 177–204.

Julian's desecration of the body of St. Babilas took place near Antioch, where a Christian church had been built near a pagan temple. As a result of the ensuing rivalry between Christian and pagan communities, the gods of this temple soon ceased to pronounce their oracles. This failure was distressing to Julian, and when he was told that it had resulted from contamination of the site by dead Christian bodies, especially that of St. Babilas, he took prompt action. Unceremoniously, he had the saint's remains removed from the church, placed in a wagon, and carted away to a distant cemetery. Following the wagon was a large crowd of angry Christians, singing psalms, and Julian had many of them arrested. A little afterward, the pagan temple caught fire (almost certainly by accident) and it burned to the ground. Julian blamed the Christians and immediately started what promised to become a full-scale persecution. He destroyed several chapels containing martyrs' bodies, and closed the principal Christian church of Antioch after desecrating its altar and sacred vessels. Shortly thereafter he was called to the battlefield, where he died within six months (Ricciotti, 210–13).

"You have filled the whole earth . . ." The Emperor Julian in his treatise, *Against the Galileans,* quoted from Fremantle, 262.

"It is not possible to lay down . . ." Trajan to Pliny the Younger in A.D. 112, quoted from Barry, 76.

"We will not fail to explain . . ." Justin Martyr, *First Apology,* quoted from Barry, 34–36.

The later investigations of Prandi in the small anteroom (designated tomb R^1 in the technical literature) succeeded in uncovering much of interest about the structure, but nothing which could confirm or deny the theory of its use as a baptistry. Only the lower portions of the lateral walls remain, making it impossible to decide what may have been the interior arrangements for access to the reservoir. One of the surprises turned up was a small hidden underground chamber, empty when found, whose purpose is still not clear. Of equal interest is Prandi's independent and carefully measured opinion that the room R^1 was built separately, at about the same time as the red wall complex. (Prandi, *La Zona,* 30–36, and see the section of illustrations for an interesting series of photographs and cutaway sketches.)

The Tropaion as an altar: Polycarp of Smyrna, a year or so before his martyrdom in A.D. 156, paid a well-known visit to Rome to confer with Pope Anicetus on church affairs. An interesting item in the old documents concerning this visit may hold some hidden reference to the Tropaion, perhaps just then completed. The Pope, it is said, "made way for Polycarp to celebrate the Eucharist in his church, by way of doing him honor" (Letter of

Irenaeus to Pope Victor, in Eusebius, *History of the Church*, quoted from Jurgens, 106). Now a simple invitation to celebrate mass would hardly in itself have conveyed any signal honor on the famed and revered Polycarp, who must, in any case, have expected to continue his customary observance while in the city. But an invitation to officiate at the newly built Tropaion, above the very bones of Peter, would have provided the Smyrnan bishop with a moment never to be forgotten.

The first actual church: In the beginning, of course, there were no buildings specially built as churches by Christians. Everywhere, ceremonies were conducted in private homes, some of which might have a room set aside for the purpose. The earliest actual church building so far discovered is a Christian chapel found in the ruins of Dura Europos, datable to the early third century, perhaps A.D. 230. The red wall complex predates this structure by some seventy or eighty years.

More problematic is the early church structure known to have stood on the site of the Cenacle in Jerusalem. Traditionally referred to as "the mother of all the churches," it certainly dates to A.D. 120 at the latest and thus precedes the red wall complex by at least thirty years. But it may have been a private home converted to church use, not an original church building. Still, the question remains open, and perhaps can never be settled. The reference in early Syrian literature to a second-century "Christian temple" at Edessa is taken by some to record the first true church building in Christendom. But this case also is injudicable.

Peter's grave prior to the Tropaion: If the conclusions reached herein concerning the red wall complex are correct—that the area served as Christendom's first real church building and, taken as the seat of a bishop, a cathedral—it may be asked whether similar ceremonial use was made of Peter's grave in the obscure ninety or so years that preceded erection of the Tropaion. To that question the Emperor Julian provides the only clue with his remark, already quoted, that the grave even during the first period was being venerated, though "secretly." Before A.D. 125, approximately, there were no large mausoleums on the

Vatican hillside to shield the gravesite from view, so it is improbable that crowds of Christians congregated there. But it is not unlikely that the popes themselves, with a few church officials, may have conducted small Sabbath services at the grave by night. If so, then it may be said that mass has been regularly celebrated over Peter's body through an unbroken span of more than nineteen hundred years, beginning perhaps from the day of his death.

APPENDIX C

Selected Bibliography

1. PRIMARY

BARRY, C., ed., *Readings in Church History*, vol. 1, Westminster, Md., Newman Press, 1960.

BASSO, M., *Simbologia escatologica nella Necropoli Vaticana*, Vatican City, Tipografia Poliglotta Vaticana, 1981.

BELVEDERI, G., "La tomba di san Pietro e i recenti lavori nelle Grotte Vaticane," *Bolletino degli Amici Catacombe*, XIII, 1943, 1–16.

CARDINI, L., "Risultato dell'esame osteologico dei resti scheletrici di animali," in M. Guarducci, *Le Reliquie di Pietro* (see below), 161–68.

CORRENTI, V., "Relazione dello studio compiuto su tre gruppi di resti scheletrici umani già rinvenuti sotto la confessione della Basilica Vaticana," in M. Guarducci, *Le Reliquie di Pietro* (see below), 83–160.

Esplorazioni sotto la Confessione di san Pietro in Vaticano, Prepared and edited by B. M. Appolonj-Ghetti, Antonio Ferrua, Enrico Josi, Engelbert Kirschbaum, 2 vols., illus., Vatican City, Tipografia Poliglotta Vaticana, 1951 (the official report of the excavations, 1939–49).

FERRUA, A., "Nelle Grotte di san Pietro," *La Civiltà Cattolica,* XCII, 1941, 358–65, 424–33.

——, "Nuove scoperte sotto san Pietro," *La Civiltà Cattolica,* XCII, 1942, 73–86, 228–41.

——, "Sulle orme san Pietro," *La Civiltà Cattolica,* XCIV, 1943, 81–102.

——, "La storia del sepolcro di san Pietro," *La Civiltà Cattolica,* CIII, 1952, 15–29.

——, "Il sepolcro di san Pietro e di certo nella Basilica Vaticana," *Il Messaggero,* 16 January 1952.

——, "La crittografia mistica ed i graffiti Vaticana," *Rivista di Archeologia Cristiana,* XXXV, 1959, 231–47.

FREMANTLE, A., ed., *A Treasury of Early Christianity,* New York, The Viking Press, 1953.

GRISAR, H., *La Tombe Apostoliche di Roma,* Rome, Tipografia Vaticana, 1892.

——, *Analecta Romana,* vol. 1, 1899.

GUARDUCCI, M., *Cristo e san Pietro in un documento preconstantiniano della Necropoli Vaticana,* Rome, Bretschneider, 1953.

——, *I Graffiti sotto La Confessione di san Pietro in Vaticana,* 3 vols., illus., Vatican City, Libreria Editrice Vaticana, 1957.

——, *The Tomb of St. Peter* (trans. from the Italian), New York, Hawthorn Books, 1960.

——, "Il fenomino orientale dal simbolismo alfabetico e i svoi svilluppi nel mondo cristiano d'occidente," *Accademia Nazionale dei Lincei,* Quad. 62, 1964, 467–97.

——, *Le Reliquie di Pietro,* Vatican City, Libreria Editrice Vaticana, 1965.

——, *Le Reliquie di Pietro: una messa a punto,* Rome, Coletti Editore, 1967.

——, "Infundate riserve sulle Reliquie di Pietro," *Archeologia Classica,* II, 1968, 352–73.

——, *St. Pierre Retrouvé* (trans. from the Italian), Paris, Éditions St. Paul, 1974.

——, *Dal gioco letterale alla crittografia mistica,* Berlin, Walter de Gruyter, 1978.

——, *La Capsella Eburnea di Samagher*, Società Istriana Archeologia e Storia Patria, 1978.

HOWE, G., and HARRER, G. A., eds., *Roman Literature in Translation*, New York, Harper & Brothers, 1952.

JAMES, M. R., *The Apocryphal New Testament*, London, Oxford University Press, 1953.

JOSI, E., "Gli scavi nelle Sacre Grotte Vaticana," *Il Vaticano nel 1944*, Rome, 1945, 2–13.

JURGENS, W., ed., *The Faith of the Early Fathers*, vol. I, Collegeville, Minnesota, The Liturgical Press, 1970.

KAAS, L., (untitled report on the excavations under St. Peter's) *Life* magazine, 27 March 1950. (Kaas' text is part of an illustrated article entitled, "The Search for the Bones of St. Peter," but the article has nothing to say about Peter's remains. In his text Kaas explains, "For the time being the discoveries which were made in the central area below the main altar of St. Peter's must remain undisclosed," and he says that an official report would soon be forthcoming. This was *Esplorazioni*, etc., see above.)

KIRSCHBAUM, E., "Gli scavi sotto la Basilica di San Pietro," *Gregorianum*, XXIX, 1948, 544–57.

——, *The Tombs of St. Peter and St. Paul* (trans. from the German), New York, St. Martin's Press, 1959.

——, "The Tomb of St. Peter," in C. Hollis, *The Papacy* (see below), 10–21.

——, "Zu den Neuesten Entdeckungen unter der Peterskirche in Rom," *Archivum Historiae Pontificiae*, 3, 1965, 309–16.

LAURO, C., and NEGRETTI, G., "Risultate dell'analisi petrografica dei Campioni di Terra," in M. Guarducci, *Le Reliquie di Pietro* (see above), 169–81.

PRANDI, A., *La Zona Archeologica della Confessio Vaticana*, Vatican City, Tipografia Poliglotta Vaticana, 1957.

RESPIGHI, C., "Esplorazioni recenti nella Confessione Beati Petri," *Rivista di Archeologia Cristiana* XIX, 1942, 19–26.

——, "La Tomba Apostolica del Vaticano," *Rivista di Archeologia Cristiana*, XIX, 1943, 5–27.

STEIN, M., and MALATESTA, P., "Risultato del'esame merceologico dei frammenti di tessuti," in M. Guarducci, *Le Reliquie di Pietro* (see above), 182–85.

TOYNBEE, J., "The Shrine of St. Peter and Its Setting," *Journal of Roman Studies*, XLIII, 1953, 1–26.

——, and PERKINS, J. W., *The Shrine of St. Peter and the Vatican Excavations*, New York, Pantheon Books, 1957.

2. SECONDARY

CARCOPINO, J., "Les Fouilles de St. Pierre et la Tradition," in *Études d'histoire chrétienne*, Paris, Éditions Albin/Michel, 1963.

COPPO, A., "Il problema della reliquie di san Pietro," *Rivista di Storia e Letterature Religiosa* I, 1965, 424–32.

CULLMANN, O., *Peter: Disciple, Apostle, Martyr* (trans. from the German), 2nd ed., Philadelphia, Westminster Press, 1962.

GIORDANI, I., *The Social Message of the Early Church Fathers* (trans. from the Italian), Boston, St. Paul Editions, 1977.

HERTLING, L., and KIRSCHBAUM, E., *The Roman Catacombs and Their Martyrs* (trans. from the German), Darton, Longman & Todd, London, 1960.

HOLLIS, C., ed., *The Papacy*, New York, The Macmillan Company, 1964.

HUDEC, L., "Recent Excavations Under St. Peter's," *Journal of the Bible and Religion*, II, 1952, 13–18.

JOURNET, C., *The Primacy of Peter* (trans. from the French), Westminster, Md., Newman Press, 1954.

LEES-MILNE, J., *Saint Peter's: The Story of Saint Peter's Basilica in Rome*, Boston, Little, Brown and Company, 1967.

MENEN, A., "St. Peter's," *National Geographic*, December 1971, 865–79.

——, *Upon This Rock*, New York, Saturday Review Press, 1972.

MORHMANN, C., "A propos de deux mots controversés de la latine chrétienne—Tropaeum—nomen," *Vigiliae Christianae*, VIII, 1964, 154–73.

o'callaghan, r., "Recent Excavations Under the Vatican Crypt," *The Biblical Archaeologist*, XII, 1949, 1–23.

——, "The Vatican Excavations and the Tomb of St. Peter," *The Biblical Archaeologist*, XVI, 1953, 70–87.

o'connell, b., "St. Peter's Bones—Are They or Aren't They?" *Science Digest*, December 1968, 7–12.

o'connor, d. w., *Peter in Rome: The Literary, Liturgical, and Archaeological Evidence*, New York, Columbia University Press, 1969.

o'dougherty, e., "The Tomb of St. Peter," *American Ecclesiastical Review*, January–June 1952, 438–44.

parrot, a., *Golgotha and the Church of the Holy Sepulchre* (trans. from the French), New York, Philosophical Library, 1957.

ricciotti, g., *Julian the Apostate* (trans. from the Italian), Milwaukee, Bruce Publishing Co., 1960.

ruysschaert, j., "The Tomb of St. Peter," *Thought*, XXIV, 1963, 5–15.

——, "Concernant La Tombe de Pierre au Vatican," *Revue d'histoire ecclésiastique*, 60, 1965, 822–32.

smothers, e., "The Excavations Under St. Peter's," *Theological Studies*, XVII, 1956, 293–321.

——, "The Bones of St. Peter," *Theological Studies*, XXVII, 1966, 79–88.

torp, h., "The Vatican Excavations and the Cult of St. Peter," *Acta Archaeologica*, XXIV, 1953, 27–66.

toynbee, j., "Graffiti Beneath St. Peter's: Dr. Guarducci's Interpretation," *Dublin Review*, Autumn 1959, 234–44.

——, "Relics of St. Peter," *The Month*, June 1965, 351–57.

INDEX

A

A (Christ) monogram, 93, 94, 95
AAA (Holy Trinity) monogram, 94–95, 96
Accademia Nazionale dei Lincei, 161, 180
Acts of the Apostles, x, 34, 174
Acts of St. Peter, second-century apocryphal book, 37
Aebutius family tomb, 24
Aelius Isidorus inscription, 54, 55, 56
Aemelia Gorgonia tomb, 11–12
Against the Galileans (Julian the Apostate), 172, 176
Agiulph (deacon), 157
Agricola. *See* Flavius Agricola tomb
Alcestis, 23
Alley (alleyway), St. Peter's Basilica, 63, 65, 81, 143, 144, 145; sketch reconstruction of, 68, 143
Alphabetical symbolism, 93–98
Alpha-omega (AO) monogram, 93–94
Anacletus, Pope, 37, 67, 156
Analecta Romana (Grisar), 157, 180
Angelis d'Ossat, Guglielmo de, 168
Anicetus, Pope, 67, 156, 176–77; and the Tropaion as an altar, 176–77
Anima dulcis Gorgonia inscription, 12
Animal bones, 103, 104, 105, 106, 110, 112, 114–15, 129
Ankh, 85
Anterooms, St. Peter's Basilica, 63, 64, 68, 176

Antioch, 34; church of, 175–76; Peter at, 34
Antoninus Pius, Emperor, 66, 140, 141
AO (alpha-omega) monogram, 93–94
Apocalypse, St. John's, 93
Apocryphal writings, details of Peter's burial in, 37
Apollo Harpocrates, 154
Appolonj-Ghetti, Bruno, 17, 179
Architecture, funerary, 13, 69, 133. *See also* Pagan funerary architecture and tombs; specific aspects, developments, events, kinds, tombs
Archivum Historiae Pontificiae, 168, 181
Arianism, 175
Augustus, Emperor, coin of, 62

B

Babilas, St., 175–76
Baptism ceremony, 138, 144–46
Baptistry, 143
Barry, C., 171, 176, 179
Beccati, Giovanni, 168
Belvederi, G., 158, 179
Birds, tomb depictions of, 23
Bishops, "burial grounds for," 65, 67
Bone depositories (ossuariums), 27
Bonifatia (Latin inscription), 47
Book of the Popes (*Liber Pontificalis*), 67, 155, 156, 173
Bronze sarcophagus, St. Peter's, 30, 37–38, 71, 155, 156; gold lining, 30